MANAGEMENT OF INNOVATION IN

THE NEW MILLENNIUM

MANAGEMENT OF INNOVATION IN THE NEW MILLENNIUM

D. Bruce Merrifield
CEO, Pridco Management Corp.
Prof. Of Management, Emeritus
Wharton Business School

© Copyright 2000, Bruce Merrifield

All rights reserved.
No part of this book may be reproduced, stored in a retrieval system, or transmitted by any means, electronic, mechanical, photocopying, recording, or otherwise, without written permission from the author.

ISBN: 1-58721-507-1

PREFACE

THE REMARKABLE ERA IN WHICH WE LIVE

The last chaotic years of the 20th Century now are seeing a largely unanticipated and little appreciated confluence of three independent phenomena, each of significant magnitude. Combined, they are causing unprecedented degrees of economic and social turbulence, that will continually compound the difficulties of all forms of management. New skills, concepts and disciplines, known but not widely practiced, will be required to cope with the discontinuities that are resulting.

One of these phenomena involves an explosive advance of technology, which already has collapsed product and life cycles form decades to just a few years in many industries, obsoleting equipment and facilities long before their useful lives can be realized. A second involves the coincidental end of a fourth 50 year economic cycle, the last stages of which always have been marked by a worldwide glut of capacity in many commodity businesses. This excess capacity now must be significantly cut back, and the businesses involved must be downsized and restructured...a process well advanced in the U.S. but not in other countries. Serious unemployment and social unrest likely will result.

The third phenomena has resulted primarily from extraordinary advances in communications which recently have tied the world together, for the first time...in real time. Thousands of cross border alliances now are forming which are bypassing regulatory, language, and cultural barriers, and also are rapidly eroding the financial and economic sovereignty of the Nation State system. In fact, this period now is seeing the last stages of a 6th great 500 year Epoch, now going to 1000 B.C. An "older order," the Nation State system, is giving way to a "new order," a Global Village without boarders. The last century of each of these 500 year Epochs has always involved massive trauma and turbulence...wars, the collapse of empires, and economic restructuring. This 20th century has already seen unparalleled turbulence, which may escalate further.

- Organizations caught in the down draft of a collapsing Order, may not survive, but that those that catch the rising tide of a new Order can flourish.

Unfortunately, the combined effect of these three phenomena (each of historic significance in its own right), have not only exponentially increased the level of global turbulence, but also have collapsed the time frame for adjustment to an unprecedented degree.

THE CHANGING NATURE OF MANAGEMENT

From a management point of view, corporate survival now requires an intensively focused process of continuous renewal. Former strategies that previously were successful, no longer will suffice. Survival cannot be assured by being a low cost producer of a commodity awash in excess capacity. Also, survival can no longer be assured by simply making incremental annual improvements in existing operations. Instead, discovery, development, scale-up, production, and worldwide marketing of next-generation systems increasingly will be required.

BENEFICIARIES OF THIS BOOK

- SCIENTISTS AND ENGINEERS

  The engineering and science curricula in our universities do not provide much of an insight into the multiple step, complex, interactive, distributed, and non-linear process of innovation, which is required for translating a basic research discovery into a marketable product, process or service. Nor do these curricula provide insight into measuring the probability of commercial success for an earlier stage development. As a result, the shelves of many research laboratories are cluttered with partially developed products and processes that probably should not have been started. The efficiency of R&D can be very significantly increased, by the use of effective metrics, and by the acquisition of the special skills now needed to manage in the new millennium.

o BUSINESS MANAGERS

Evaluation metrics are needed for business managers both for benchmarking existing operations against world competition, and for evaluating opportunities for new investments of all kinds. In addition, a growing need now exists for assembling, coordinating and integrating various forms of collaborative efforts, often in some sort of "virtual" organization, an important specialized discipline, not generally taught.

o FINANCIAL ANALYSTS

The "constraint and sensitivity" forms of business analysis combined with S-curve simulations and projections of past trends, can be powerful tools for making both short and longer term investments. A clearer understanding of the nature of the innovation process, and of the incremental process of risk reduction that is involved, also can be helpful.

o MBA STUDENTS

This book originally was developed for new courses in both Entrepreneurship and The Management of Innovation, in the Center for Entrepreneurship at the Wharton School of Business at the University of Pennsylvania. Entrepreneurship is a very rapidly growing subject area in almost all business schools, reflecting the "American Miracle" which was jump-started by the Economic Recovery Act of 1981, and since has been augmented by much additional legislation. It could have additional use in a number of other schools.

AUTHOR BACKGROUND

The author has been in research and research administration fro many years, and formerly was Vice President of Technology for both the Occidental Petroleum Company, and the Continental Group, (Continental Can Co.). Since then, Dr. Merrifield has headed up the Technology Administration in the Reagan Administration, where he put through landmark legislation to change the antitrust laws and to allow collaborative research and production efforts among U.S. companies. His office also put through the Technology Transfer Acts of 1984, 1986, and 1989 which for the first time made available Federally funded research for industrial development. Other legislation included the Technology Medal, the Baldridge Quality Award, the Patent Extension Act, which starts the 17 year meter running only after regulatory clearance has been received; and the Process Patent Act, which protects U.S. process patents from foreign infringement. His office also initiated the R&D Limited Partnership model for collaborative efforts, including Sematech, which had its origin in his office; and the International Program for Acceleration of Commercial Technology (INPACT), which established collaborative arrangements between the U.S. and developing countries, to develop new entrepreneurial businesses. Dr. Merrifield is Professor Emeritus of the Wharton School of Business, where he held the Walter Bladstrom Chair for Entrepreneurship, and currently is the Chairman and CEO of two privately held new ventures.

FORWARD

Since 1000 B.C, civilization has sequentially passed through six great 500 year epochs, the most recent of which is now coming to an end. Remarkably, only at each 500 year node has each old order been destroyed and a new order emerged. The last epoch which began in 1500 A.D. resulted in the destruction of the 500 year Feudal era, and the onset of The Renaissance. It also ushered in our current Nation State system.

Importantly, the last century in each epoch, has always been one of great turmoil and upheaval, and this pattern now is repeating right on schedule. In fact, this last 100 years has been one of unparalleled upheaval, involving two world wars, separated by the Great Depression, the concurrent collapse of all the colonial empires, a 50 year "cold" war, and the current violent ethnic "balkanization" and terrorism of many disintegrating countries.

Even more important, and perhaps still inadequately appreciated, is the fact that the last 30 years of this 500 year epoch now has seen the generation of about 90% of all known scientific knowledge --- produced by about 90% of all the scientists and engineers who have ever lived, and now are living and working. This historically unprecedented phenomenon, already has collapsed product and process life cycles from decades to just a few years in many industries, obsolescing equipment and facilities long before their useful lives can be realized. It has abruptly tied the world together in real time, and simultaneously initiated thousands of cross-border alliances that are bypassing regulatory, language and cultural barriers. As a result, we now are seeing the progressive erosion of both the economic and financial sovereignty of the Nation State system, and the emergence of a global village without economic borders.

Management in this era of unprecedented change now has become the management of change and renewal, focused around the need for continuous innovation. The basic reality, is that corporate survival no longer can be assured by being a low cost producer of a commodity in a world awash in excess capacity, or only by making incremental improvements in existing operations. Instead, survival, let alone profitable growth, now will require developing and sustaining a significant competitive advantage, based on ownership or timely access to knowledge-intensive, high value-added, proprietary operations.

The process of management involved, increasingly will require the real-time integration of technical, legal, financial, marketing and production capabilities. The skills and disciplines required are better known than widely practiced or taught, and often will involve vertically integrated arrangements on a global scale. This book describes the essential elements involved in the management of innovation from initial discovery to commercial operation. It explains the metrics for valuation of existing businesses and new opportunities, in a methodology that usually results in 8 or 9 out of 10 successes. It further develops the pros and cons of alternative legal forms of organization and of strategic alliances. Finally it describes the avoidable failure modes that can beset these novel but necessary structures, which increasingly can spell the difference between success and failure.

CONTENTS

PREFACE   v

FORWARD   ix

Chapter I A Global Perspective

- The Changing Nature of Competitive Advantage 1
- Failed Strategies 3
- The Kondratieff Longwave 6
- Important Concepts to Review 10
- References 12

Chapter II Forces of Change Restructuring World Econonmies

- Perspective 13
- The Critical Technologies 15
- Critical Material-Science Technologies 17
- Critical Technologies Involved in Electronics and Information Systems 19
- Critical Energy Technologies 21
- The Bio-Sciences 22
- Critical Technologies Involved in Engineering and Manufacturing 23
- Important Concepts to Review 25

Chapter III Innovation Metrics, Constraint Analysis

- Perspective 27
- The Six Business Attractiveness Factors 31
  - Sales, Profit Potential 31
  - Growth Potential 33
  - The Competitive Environment Factor 36
  - Risk Distribution Factor 41
  - Opportunity to Restructure an Industry 43
  - Political and Social Constraints 45
- Six Business "Fit" Factors 47
  - Capital Availability 47
  - Marketing and Distribution Requirements 49

- o Manufacturing Capabilities 51
- o Technology Support Function 52
- o Access to Critical Materials and Components 54
- o Management Competence 55
- o Regression Analysis Data 57
- o References 63
- o Key Concepts to Review 64

Chapter VI Sensitivity Analysis

- o Perspective 65
- o The Sensitivity Analysis 67
- o Productivity Measurements 69
- o Market Valuations and Simulations 72
- o Other Simulations 73
- o Summary 76
- o References 77
- o Key Concepts to Review 78

Chapter V Innovation Driven Continuous Corporate Renewals

- o Perspective 79
- o Life Cycle Patterns 80
- o Forecasting The Future 84
  - o The Future of Education 85
  - o The Future of Communications 87
  - o Information Technology (IT) 89
  - o Medicine and Biogenetics 91
  - o Banking and Financial Services 93
- o Steps Involved in Continuous Renewal 94
- o The Strategic Plan 97
- o The Business Plan 100
- o Summary 103
- o References 104
- o Key Concepts to Review 105

Chapter VI Management of the Technical Function   107

- o Perspective 107
- o The Innovation Process 108
- o Advisory Boards 112

- o   Flexible Computer-Integrated Manufacturing 113
- o   Intellectual Property Management 115
- o   Personnel Management, and Technology Audits.... 116
- o   Environmental Audit.. 119
- o   Summary 121
- o   References 122
- o   Key Concepts to Review... 123

Chapter VII Legal Forms of Organization and Strategic Alliance

- o   Perspective 125
- o   Alternative Forms of Organization 127
- o   The Limited Liability Corporation........................... 130
- o   Failure Modes for Collaborative Efforts.................. 132
- o   A Modern Marshall Plan for Developing Economies "INPACT" Organizations 133
- o   Summary 137
- o   References 138
- o   Important Concepts to Review................................ 139

Chapter VIII A Global Village in the Third Millennium   141

- o   Perspective 141
- o   Disruptive Monetary and Fiscal Policies 143
- o   Breaking the Cycle.. 146
- o   The Emerging Global Village 151
- o   Summary 153
- o   References 154
- o   Key Concepts to Review... 155

Appendix I A Summary of 500 Year Epochs   157

Appendix II Regression Analysis Data for Monetary
    Interventions   160

Appendix III Background on the Federal Reserve 164

CHAPTER I

A GLOBAL PERSPECTIVE

The Changing Nature of Competitive Advantage

No organization has an inalienable right to survive in the current hyper-competitive global marketplace, with its rapidly vanishing borders. In fact, about 70% of the companies originally listed in the "Fortune 500," no longer are listed there. Unfortunately, more famous corporate names likely will disappear over the next decade, even though this could be avoided. Moreover, the consequences of their demise have been profound.

- Since 1982, about 40 million jobs have been lost through downsizing, reengineering, liquidations and takeovers. This is more than were lost even in the Great Depression of the 1930's.
- Fortunately, this devastating loss, which should have precipitated another severe depression, was more than offset by the simultaneous creation of about 75 million new jobs (Figure 1), most of them in millions of new small businesses, which also were formed since 1982. Over 50% of the new jobs which have been generated, also have been high-paying professional, technical, and managerial in nature.

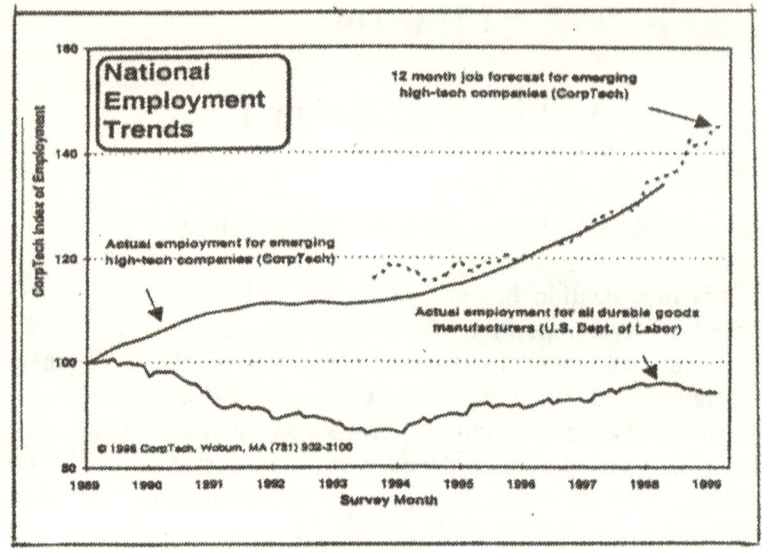

Figure 1

A remarkable entrepreneurial revolution has been responsible for this phenomenon --- one that has been unique to the United States and is historically unprecedented in scope and significance. Europeans call it the "American Miracle." In principle, the process involved can be replicated anywhere, or within any organization, provided an appropriate environment for risk investments and high level support is created and sustained. Several very successful pilot models already exist in India (the "PACT" program), in Israel (the BIRD Foundation) and in France (The FACET program), which could be widely replicated particularly in many other developing countries.

Moreover, industrial survival, let alone profitable long term growth, now will depend increasingly on the adoption of strategies that can both develop and sustain a "meaningful" competitive advantage. Unfortunately, many strategies that have been successful in the past, no longer are viable.

Failed Strategies

For many centuries, economic advantage, between warring fiefdoms or nation states, primarily depended upon ownership of, (or forced access to), arable land, natural resources, and waterways for trade. The recent revolutions in transportation, communications, flexible manufacturing, and agriculture, have mitigated these needs. Moreover, capital and information now flow with the speed of light anywhere in the world, bypassing regulatory, language and cultural barriers. Also, cross-border alliances, and financial manipulation of world exchange and interest rates, now are rapidly eroding both the financial and economic sovereignty of the nation state system.

Consequently, obsolescent businesses can no longer hide, for long, behind protective Government tariffs and quotas. Moreover, an alternative strategy of being a low-cost producer of commodity products -- in a world awash in excess capacity --- is not a recipe for survival. Neither will it suffice any more, to only make incremental improvements, each year, in existing operations, although these will always be necessary. Instead, significant investments also must be made in cutting-edge, next-generation systems, which are deliberately designed to continually obsolete current investments.

A cornerstone of understanding must recognize that rapidly advancing technology now has collapsed product and process life cycles from decades to just a few years in many industries. As a result, existing facilities and equipment can become obsolescent long before their useful lives can be realized --- or even fully paid for. Moreover, the "core competencies" that manage them can become equally obsolescent. Therefore, a sustainable competitive advantage now requires a disciplined process of continuous innovation and corporate renewal, incentivized for risk investments.

In the 1970's and early 1980's, the Japanese developed, what seemed at that time, to be a remarkable model for achieving an unsurmountable competitive advantage. It was based on the Boston Consulting Group (BCG) "fast-follower, Government-subsidized, learning-curve" theory. BCG had observed that, on average, every doubling of industry volume, reduced operating costs 20% or more. Therefore, a new competitor could rapidly capture an existing market by pricing (point 4, in Figure 2), well below existing competitor's costs (points 1,2, 3). The negative cash flow that resulted, was (1) Government subsidized by providing zero real interest rates, (2) by special subsidies, (3) by closing off imports so domestic prices could be maintained higher than those for export (now called dumping), and (4) by forgiving the value-added tax for exports. This strategy was enormously successful in in the 1970's and early 1980's, when Japan captured major market shares, for example, in steel, shipbuilding, consumer electronics, machine tools, robots, textiles, shoes, plastics and by 1984, about 90% of the semiconductor mass-memory business.

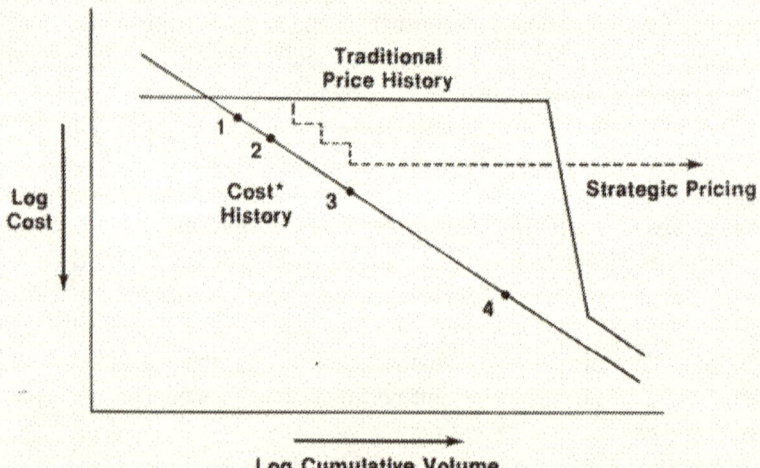

Figure 2

However, the fallacy in this "zero-sum, beggar thy neighbor" strategy, is that it assumes that the products which are targeted, and the facilities to make them, will have sufficiently long lives, both to first capture the market from competitors, and then to recover the accrued debts. Moreover, when all the other Asian nations copied this tempting model, an enormous glut of capacity resulted. China and other Asian countries, currently are operating below 50% of rated capacity and often are pricing exports below actual costs. Writing off these now rapidly obsolescing facilities, and restructuring the enormous debts involved may take a number of years --- a primary cause of the Asian meltdown, and also European unemployment. The urgent need now is to adopt already proven strategies that create many new entrepreneurial businesses, and new jobs, to offset the downsizing process. A basic understanding is that technology has become the primary engine of growth and prosperity. Consequently, corporate survival increasingly will depend upon the effective discovery, development, scale-up, production and marketing of a never-ending stream of cutting-edge next-generation products, processes, and services. Several basic realities now are apparent:

o Wealth no longer will be measured in terms of ownership of rapidly obsolescing fixed physical assets.
o Wealth, instead, now will be measured primarily in terms of ownership of (or time-critical access to) knowledge-intensive, high value-added, strongly-proprietary, technology-based systems.
o Management, therefore, has become the management of continuous change, and any organization not involved in a process of continuous renewal, likely has made an unintentional decision not to survive for long.

Unfortunately, few organizations, alone, can hold captive all the continuously changing skills and resources needed both to improve existing operations each year, and to simultaneously develop next-generation systems. Consequently, collaborative efforts increasingly will be required, even though those involve management disciplines better understood than widely practiced. Moreover, the current global glut of capacity that exists in many commodity businesses, now must be written down with serious losses of jobs, and needs to be offset with an entrepreneurial process in other countries comparable to the American Miracle. In fact, the "Asia meltdown" is the last phase of the well understood "Kondratieff Longwave."

The Kondratieff Longwave

Nikolai Kondratieff, a Russian economist, was the Director of the Institute of Economic Research in Moscow, during the early 1920's. In 1925, he put forward an hypothesis that contradicted the Marxist assertion that the capitalist countries would self-destruct. Instead, he pointed out that these countries on average fell into severe depressions every 54 years, and he predicted that the next depression would occur in the 1930's. His thesis was very controversial, and for his insight, he was exiled to a Siberian salt mine where he died in 1937. More recently the Longwave has been further documented by Jay Forrester at MIT and others. Joseph Schumpeter has noted that each longwave begins with a spurt of technological innovation.

Currently we are seeing the last phase of the 4th longwave, now going back 200 years. Moreover, this is the last one, since product and process life cycles now have collapsed to just a few years. Forrester has identified four phases in each 50 year cycle (Figure 3):

- o The first phase is a 15-year period of collapse, in which many obsolescent facilities in over-capacity are written down, taken over, or go into bankruptcy. However, by the end of this period, pent up demands stimulates a second-phase 20 year period of reinvestment, building on latent technology that had been rejected in the previous longwave. A third 10 year phase follows, in which excess capacity again is built, and the fourth phase is a period of economic turbulence with erosion of profitability, slow growth, and deepening recession cycles, before the next collapse occurs.

The Kondratieff Longwave

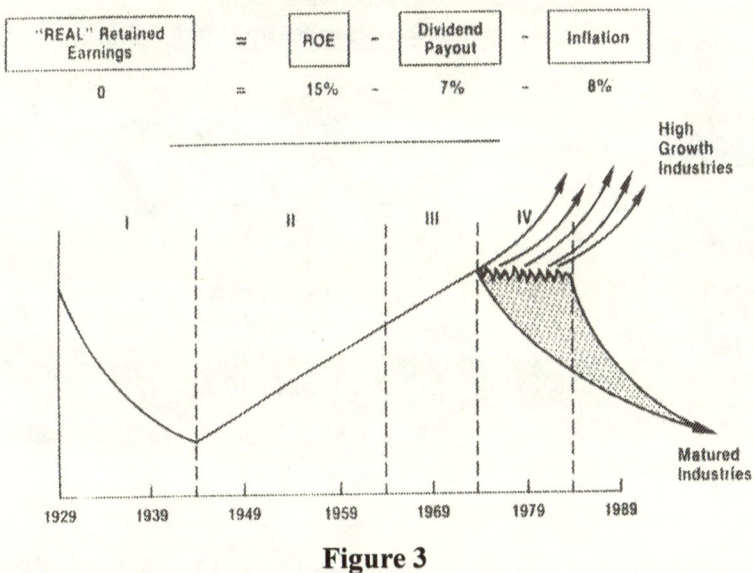

Figure 3

o   The last longwave began with the 1929 market crash and the first phase lasted until 1945. However, World War II had jump-started the development of previously discovered advanced systems (radar, penicillin, the sulfa drugs, color TV, the transistor, jet engines, FM radios, Xerography etc.) --- and these then fueled an enormous 20 year (1945-1965) investment period. Sales and profits grew rapidly dropping unemployment to low levels. By 1965 supply had caught up with demand, but strong cash flows sustained further investments, and by 1975 much excess capacity had developed with erosion of profits. A period of "stagflation" characterized the fourth phase between 1975 and 1985 following which the current U.S. "downsizing and reenginering" process has lost 40 million jobs. Stock market price indices nicely illustrate these four phases (Figure 4).

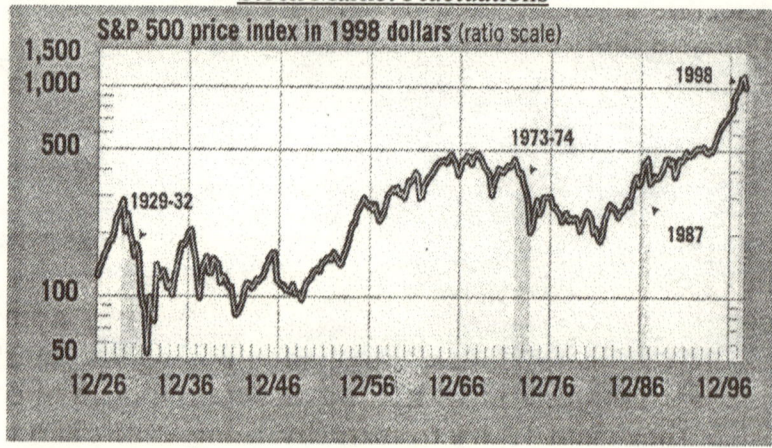

Figure 4

Fortunately, the Economic Recovery Tax Act of 1981 forestalled what should have been a serious depression. It reduced taxes by about $500 billion, and dropped the capital gains tax to 20% (which had been 70% in early 1980). This jump-started an historically unprecedented small business formation process, triggered by the rapid generation of $35 billion in venture capital that immediately followed. New U.S. incorporations doubled from about 300,000 to 600,000 and now over 800,00 per year. Stock market capitalization has increased 5 fold, more than offsetting the losses sustained in downsizing.

Unfortunately, this renewal process has lagged in Japan and Europe, and is barely beginning in most other Asian countries. Chile alone in South America, under the much reviled Pinochet, also began the renewal process in the 1980's, bringing in the University of Chicago Business School people for guidance. With markets opened for foreign investment and privatization of companies that had been nationalized by Allende, a burgeoning small business development process has created the needed economic and political support for democratic forms of governance to follow. This same process has developed in Taiwan and is beginning in South Korea, and other Asian countries. However, it needs to be accelerated, and the U.S. has a primary responsibility for leadership in its own enlightened self interest.

IMPORTANT CONCEPTS TO REVIEW

- What strategies for achieving a sustainable competitive advantage no longer will work, and which ones will?
- Why do many organizations reject new technologies that eventually bypass them, resulting in their loss of market share or even in their demise?
- What is the definition of wealth?
- Any rice paddy in the world can be transformed in less than a year to a state of the art production facility to make already existing products. Why has this strategy failed, and what would be a better strategy?
- Developing countries do not have the academic infrastructure to do basic research or develop cutting-edge advanced technologies. What strategies do they need to develop for sustainable economic growth?
- You are the CEO of a company primarily involved in several commodity businesses with few barriers to entry and with marginal, if any, competitive advantages. What would you do, first, second and third?
- What is the "paradigm shift" in management strategy now required for survival?
- Why will we never again see a Kondratieff Longwave?

Appendix I

Below is the Kondratieff Longwave extended back to 1800 showing the U.S. divergence from an expected decline.

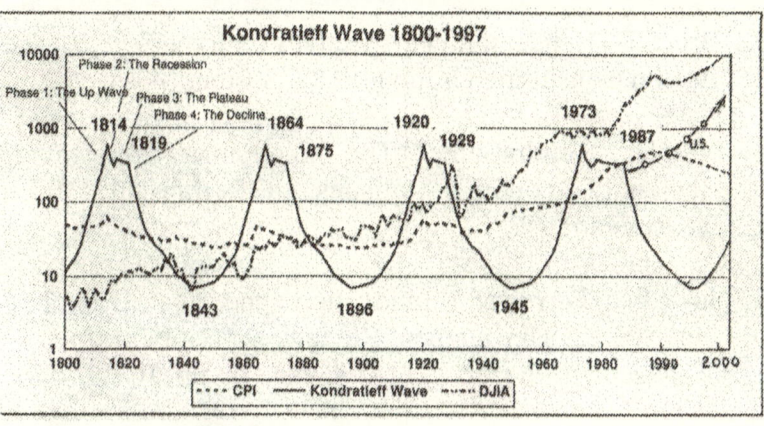

REFERENCES

1. U.S. Dept. Of Commerce, Bureau Economic Analysis, <u>Quarterly Reports</u>

2. Bruce D. Henderson "Perspectives on Experience," The Boston Consulting Group (1968), Boston, Mass.

3. Nikolai Kondratieff, "The Economic Longwave," <u>Review of Economic Statistics</u>, 1935 (translation from the Russian)

4. Jay W. Forrester "Innovation and the Economic Longwave," <u>Management Review</u>, American Management Assoc. <u>Vol. 68</u>, No. 6, pp 16-24, June 1975

5. Joseph Schumpeter

CHAPTER II

FORCES OF CHANGE RESTRUCTURING WORLD ECONOMIES

Perspective

Two primary forces of change now are restructuring all world economies, ushering in a remarkable period of political, economic, and social change. Both the scale and the rate at which these changes are occurring are historically unprecedented. One of these forces involves a demographic phenomenon, which has resulted from the stunning fall of the Berlin Wall, and the subsequent final discreditation of the Marxist-socialist paradigm. The demise of this paradigm has abruptly released over 3 billion people now to participate, for the first time, in market-based economies. These political, social, and economic changes inevitably will be accompanied by extended global turbulence, some of which already is in evidence.

The second force of change involves an equally powerful explosion of advanced technology, which is rapidly obsoleting large investments in existing facilities and equipment, before their useful lives can be realized. Technology now is the engine of industrial competitiveness, providing an overwhelming competitive advantage to those nations and organizations that can continually develop "next-generation" operations. The possibility to do this has been enormously increased by the fact that about 90% of all scientific knowledge, ever developed, has been developed over just the last 30 years (Figure 5) --- by about 90% of all the scientists and engineers who have ever lived, and now are living and working. Moreover, this scientific database, and the number of technical people, both will likely double again over the next 15 years or so. As a result, the opportunities to create new businesses and new jobs anywhere in the world is unprecedented.

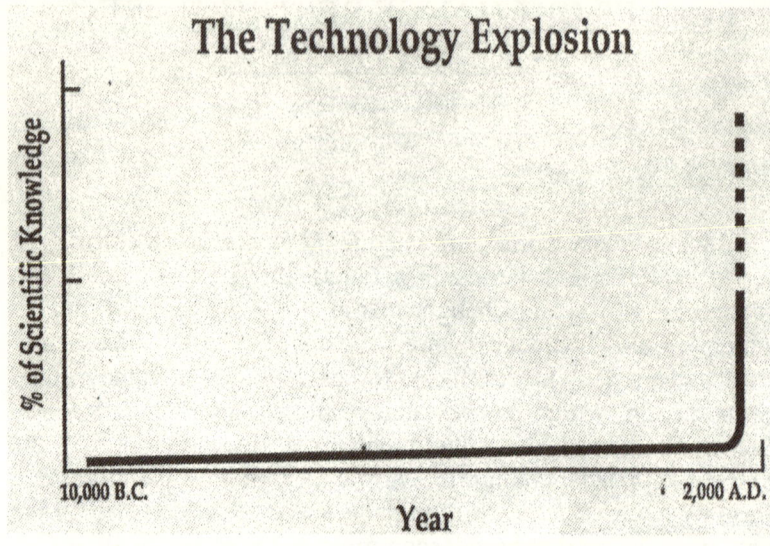

Figure 5

A multiplicity of disciplines are involved over a broad array of areas of investigation (the material sciences, the electronics and communication sciences, the biosciences, energy systems, and the manufacturing and engineering sciences). These diverse disciplines also interact with each other in unexpected ways, to produce surprise innovations, not anticipated in the original work. The current remarkable pace and scope of this phenomenon had its origin in World War II, which forced the mobilization of tremendous resources to build thousands of planes, ships, and advanced munitions, as well as penicillin, the sulfa drugs, radar --- and the atomic bomb which ended the war and stunned the world scientific community. Vannevar Bush captured the euphoria of the moment in his Presidential Report, calling "Research the Endless Frontier." As a result, the National Science Foundation was created to fund basic research, and since then about a $trillion dollars have been spent to build a unique academic infrastructure in U.S. universities and Government laboratories. Currently the U.S. spends about $220 billion each year for R&D, and $35 billion for basic research each year --- more than all other nations combined (Figure 6).

1998 Research and Development Expenditures ($Billions)

1998 Research and Development Expenditures ($Billions)

Source	Basic Research		Applied Research		Development	
	Amount	% Total	Amount	% Total	Amount	% Total
- Universities	$20.3	59%	$7.9	16%	$2.7	2%
- Industry	8.6	25%	34.9	70%	127.8	90%
- Federal	2.8	8%	5.0	10%	8.2	6%
- Non Profits	2.7	8%	2.0	4%	2.7	2%
	$34.4	100%	$49.8	100%	$136.4	100%

Source: National Science Foundation

Figure 6

As a result, the U.S. receives most of the Nobel prizes, and makes most of the seminal discoveries. These recently have led to the emergence of several dozen "critical technologies" that are so important that they likely will restructure most industries over the next decade or two, and will dominate the early 21st century.

The Critical Technologies

In previous centuries, important innovations were few and very far between, but when they did happen, they often introduced important political and social, as well as economic changes. For example, the simple invention of the stirrup, revolutionized warfare, allowing mounted knights to dominate the foot soldier. This resulted in a "serf, (hired) knight, Lord," symbiotic relationship which developed into the medieval fiefdom form of social structure. Gun power finally spelled the end of this era.

More recently, product and process life cycles have lasted for decades or more (the printing press, the cotton gin, the steam engine, the electric light, the telephone, vacuum tubes, radar, and the early transistors). Many of these still exist, but have evolved to a much more advanced stage. Others no longer exist. However, the market needs that they served still do exist, and several dozen new critical technologies now will serve them (Figure 7).

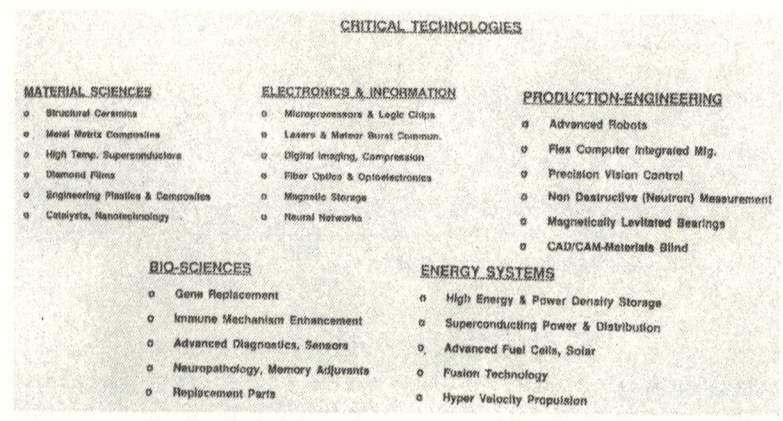

Figure 7

The surprise interaction of these technologies with each other, will continually provide unprecedented opportunities to develop new businesses, create new jobs, and expand global economies --- which still primarily involves only about 15% of world populations in already industrialized countries. Unfortunately, many bureaucratically encumbered businesses may continue to become obsolescent, and will fail to take advantage of the unprecedented opportunities now available for continuous renewal. Many more famous corporate names will continue to disappear (Swift, Packard, Westinghouse, Sinclair Oil, RCA, Firestone, U.S. Rubber, American Can, etc.).

o After World War II, Timex captured about 50% of the worldwide market for watches, by redirecting their precision manufacturing skills, (developed during the war for making fuses), into making low cost mass-produced watches, which were shock proof, had sweep second hands, and used a cheap material, (Armalloy), in place of jewels. However, the company initially rejected a new innovation in quartz crystal electronic technology --- it didn't fit their "core competency" --- and then lost the market to Japanese companies.

Sadly, this scenario will unnecessarily be repeated without a disciplined process of search and acquisition of advancing discoveries and a process of continuous innovation.

Critical Material-Science Technologies

For the first 10,000 years of recorded civilization, human creativity in this area was limited to manipulation of naturally occurring materials (copper, iron, wood, composites made from sand and gravel, amorphous silicon in the form of glass, latex from trees, and mixtures of the above). One property was traded off against another to approximate desired performance specifications. Moreover, gravity was an essential factor for the satisfactory performance of materials of construction, mobile traction and many other applications. Now, however, many such limitations have been bypassed or mitigated by an ability to design specific materials for specific applications (Figure 8).

```
           Critical Advanced-Material Technologies
  - Structural Ceramics           - Diamond Films
  - Metal Matrix Components       - Engineering Plastics & Polymer
  - Super Alloys                  - Surface-Engineered Materials
  - Magnetic & Optical Devices    - High Surface Area Particles
  - Chemically Specific Catalysts   & Coatings
  - Bioactive & Biocompatible     - High Temperature Supercon-
    Implants                        ductivity Materials
```

Figure 8

For example, High Temperature Superconducting (HTS) ceramics, now are being developed for use in motors, generators, fault current limiters, electrical energy storage and power transmission cables. HTS cables can transmit electricity with almost no losses over long distances, and when developed, likely will restructure the utility industry. Electricity generated in remote locations will be economically accessible (wind, solar, geothermal, tidal, hydroelectric, and perhaps ocean thermal). As the world moves toward an all-electric economy, even fossil fuels may be converted at the well head, or mine pit to electricity with centralized control of pollution. Russia, for example, has three major natural gas fields in Siberia, each of which is larger than all known U.S. natural gas reserves, and as yet undeveloped. Moreover, Iceland has an enormous geothermal steam potential for generating electricity, and Texas and North Dakota have enough untapped wind potential, to supply more than half the current U.S. demand for electricity, if it could be delivered economically to wherever it is needed.

In another area of potential importance, Nano technology, still in its infancy, now is providing the feasibility of assembling new materials never before known, atom by atom, to produce specifically desired characteristics. For example, a cluster of 12 silicon atoms behaves differently from a cluster of 13, almost like a new material. In the area of medical engineering, a remarkable period of cellular biogenetics and tissue engineering now is just beginning. Lab-grown bones, cartilage, skin, blood vessels, livers, pancreases, breasts, ears, fingers, nerves and tooth enamel now are in advanced testing and initial use. These and other ongoing developments in the material sciences will interact with each other in unexpected ways to continually improve the quality of human life.

Critical Technologies Involved in Electronics and Information Systems

Capital now flows with the speed of light anywhere in the world, and information follows just as quickly. However, for most of the 10,000 years of civilization, the process of communications was limited to the speed and endurance of a horse, a sailing ship, or perhaps a carrier pigeon. American Indians used smoke signals, and ships at sea used semaphore flags, but it wasn't until the pony express was started that "scheduled" distance communication was possible. The telegraph developed by Samuel Morse in 1837, and the telephone by Alexander Graham Bell in 1876 (initially as a hearing aid for his deaf wife), began the modern era of affordable long distance communication. Marconi developed the radio in 1895, and wireless communication began to tie the world together in real time.

Now the current revolution in communications is driven by rapidly increasing bandwidth (the volume of information that can be transmitted per unit of time), and by rapidly falling costs, through the use of satellites and fiber optic cables. These systems soon will obsolete $billions of dollars of investments in twisted copper wires and switching systems. However, such advances are just a few of the developments now under development (Figure 9).

Critical Electronics and Communication Technologies	
- Transistors, Microprocessors & logic chips	- Lasers & Optoelectronics
- Digital Imaging & Compression	- Fiber Optics
- Amorphous Liquid Crystal Displays	- Orbital Satellites
- Space Based Relays, Telescopes, Sensors	- Active & Passive Sensors
- High Density Magnetic and Optical Information Storage	- Modular Software
	- Neural Networks for Comm

Figure 9

This is the third Information Technology (IT) revolution in human history, the first being the invention of writing in Mesopotamia around 3000 to 4000 B.C. (Later reinvented in China about 2000 B.C.). The second revolution followed the invention of written books, also in China about 1300 B.C. and later again in Greece about 500 B.C. to chronicle Homer's epics, only recited until then. By the 1400's, some 10,000 monks in thousands of monasteries labored six days a week, copying books by hand in Latin.

However, Gutenberg's invention of the printing press in 1450 A.D. put these monks out of business, and the contemporaneous invention of engraving made illustrated books possible. The current revolution 500 years later, has in fact created a "global village" in which information now bypasses all barriers, and is rapidly eroding the economic and financial sovereignty of the nation state system.

All aspects of commerce and education will be affected. On-line shopping over the Internet for next-day delivery from the factory will obsolete many distribution and retail merchants. Access to expert legal, medical, and financial services already are available from any living room, and interactive video education systems for life-long continued reskilling will restructure many aspects of the educational system --- the schoolroom of one.

Critical Energy Technologies

Energy generation, storage and transmission comprise the three critical factors for this important economic area. A nation's quality of life is almost synonymous with the amount of energy that is used, and as the 85% of world populations outside the developed nations raise their standard of living, these factors will become even more important. Energy generation will increasingly become dependent on renewable sources of energy, alternative to more polluting fossil fuels (coal, oil and gas). Advances in wind, solar, geothermal, tidal and hydroelectric power will be needed, coupled with the superconducting transmission lines to distribute the power economically to any destination. Advanced batteries and superconducting energy storage systems, will provide off-peak storage and power conditioning, eliminating the current need for very expensive peak power generation, and allowing energy generation systems to run continuously. This will add about 20% additional capacity without additional capital investments (Figure 10).

Critical Energy Technology

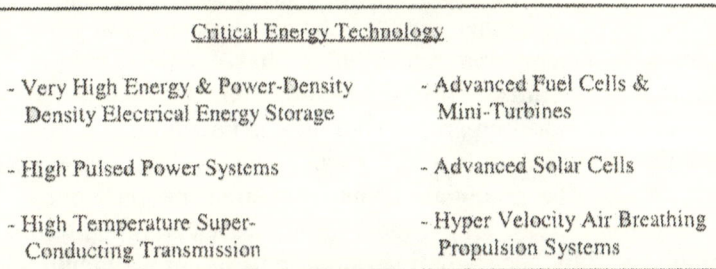

Critical Energy Technology	
- Very High Energy & Power-Density Density Electrical Energy Storage	- Advanced Fuel Cells & Mini-Turbines
- High Pulsed Power Systems	- Advanced Solar Cells
- High Temperature Super-Conducting Transmission	- Hyper Velocity Air Breathing Propulsion Systems

Figure 10

Hyper velocity propulsion systems, now in development, will telescope air travel times, and pulsed power systems (the rail gun) will radically reduce the cost of orbiting space vehicles and satellites. More efficient solar cells could make desalination of seawater economic for irrigation of desert areas.

The Bio-Sciences

For most of human history, life spans have been cut short by disease, poor nutrition, and accidents, that now are routinely cured or treatable. Herbal medicines sometimes were beneficial, and recently have been found to have a scientific basis. For example, the American Indians chewed on a bark that contained a member of the penicillin family, which now has been incorporated into a commercial toothpaste.

However, a first stage of "modern medicine" did not occur until Pasteur and others demonstrated the connection between bacteria and disease. Pasteur then produced the first cure for rabies. A more sophisticated stage of medical investigation began with Fleming's discovery of penicillin in 1928, and its commercialization during World War II. The sulfa drugs and other antibiotics followed, saving countless wounded.

Subsequent development of vaccines, heart disease drugs, and even newer antibiotics now have virtually eliminated many of the scourges of history and prolonged the life span. However, concurrent with these advances has been spectacular progress in medical engineering. Surgeons, engineers and material scientists have collaborated to provide replacement parts for hips, knees, hearts, livers and other organs. Cataract surgery, angioplasty, heart pacemakers, and defibrillators have both extended and increased the quality of life of senior citizens.

An even more remarkable era now is beginning. It involves "cellular biogenetics" and "tissue engineering," previously mentioned. The potential is one of keeping people young and healthy for a very long time. Immune rejection currently is being solved by encapsulating donor cells in porous membranes, and a universal "stem" or donor cell for all tissues now has been discovered. DNA mapping can reveal genetic deficiencies for early correction, and provide a DNA donor pool for couples desiring "designer babies," or even cloned individuals, raising serious ethical considerations never before addressed.

From an industrial point of view, the insatiable demand for a longer healthy and more "productive" life will continue to drive developments in this area. Very large increases in productivity already are resulting from the "combinatorial screening" of thousands of new chemical entities, and major advances will continue in medical and tissue engineering (Figure 11).

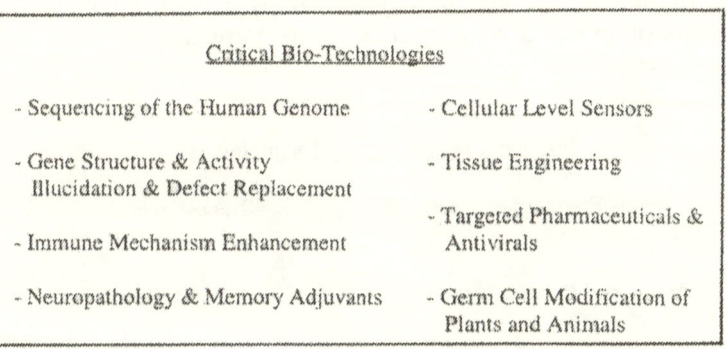

Figure 11

Critical Technologies Involved in Engineering and Manufacturing

Combinations of systems engineering, advanced materials, wireless communications, and advanced computing now are revolutionizing the manufacturing sciences. Dedicated mass production plants have become obsolescent in many industries which demand custom made products, or where advancing technology has collapsed product life cycles to just a few years. As a result, many operations have moved off-shore to low-labor cost countries. Now, however, flexible computer-integrated manufacturing (FCIM) facilities have been developed that can make one or a thousand of a kind at essentially the same cost, but also can make many custom modifications, with a few seconds turn around between kinds.

Such FCIM centers now are emerging in which a number of small companies can share time as needed for short runs and just-in-time delivery. Similar facilities can be sited around the world, and can be continually programmed and reprogrammed with changing designs by satellite from remote engineering laboratories. In joint venture relationships with companies in developing countries IS-9000 quality components can be locally provided as needed for custom assembly.

Some of the technologies that will contribute to this revolution in manufacturing include: (Figure 12)

Critical Manufacturing Technologies

- Systems Engineering Design & Management	- Nano-Level Fabrication
- Active and Passive Sensors	- Advanced Fasteners
- Vision Controlled Robots	- Artificial Intelligence
- Magnetically Levitated Bearings	- Advanced Materials Alloys and Composites

Figure 12

Barriers to realization of the inherent potential involved, lie primarily in bureaucratic systems of management that currently exist in many organizations. Corporate restructure will be required to release the latent creativity and initiative needed to realize the potential.

IMPORTANT CONCEPTS TO REVIEW

- Lesser developed countries (LDC's), which now have finally been released to participate in global markets, (but without access to cutting-edge new technologies) have therefore invested heavily in already existing technologies --- far beyond their internal needs. What strategies are needed (1) to reduce the current excess capacity, and (2) to grow those economies? Where must the leadership come from?
- A major restructure of the utility industry is in process, as deregulation allows electricity generated anywhere, to be fed into the grid, and sold anywhere bypassing currently available, and often non-competitive, generating capacity. As CEO of a utility company, what strategies would you pursue, and what kind of a business would you want to be running in 5 years?
- Any set of skills can be obsolescent in 5 to 10 years, and the great frontier of education now involves life-long reskilling. You are the President of a major university with a world-class faculty. Given the revolution in communications now in progress, what strategies would you pursue for continuing viability?
- Because of spectacular advances in the bio-sciences and medical engineering, and the coming conquest of viral mediated diseases including cancer and heart trouble, you may be able to live an active, productive life until you are at least 100 years old. Map out a personal growth strategy decade by decade.

CHAPTER III

INNOVATION METRICS, CONSTRAINT ANALYSIS

Perspective

The physicist Maxwell, was reported to have said: "if you can't measure it, you probably don't understand it." However, measuring the probability of eventual commercial success for a new venture, or a basic discovery is not easy. The difficulty is illustrated by the poor success statistics for venture capital investments. On average, 2 or 3 out of 10 such investments are successful, 2 or 3 of 10 are failures, and 4 to 6 are "walking wounded." As a result, venture capitalists often discount the net present value of potential investments by 40% or more, to compensate for those that don't succeed. Moreover, the shelves of many corporate research laboratories are cluttered with reports of partially developed products and processes, that never should have been started.

Nevertheless, industrial survival, let alone profitable growth, increasingly will depend upon making continuous risk investments, and a screening methodology that can identify those that have the highest probability of success, will become increasingly important. To this end, a regression analysis of many successful and unsuccessful ventures, has identified a dozen critical factors, which when satisfied in substantial degree, predict success 80% to 90% of the time. This methodology called the "Constraint Analysis" also is useful for measuring the continuing viability and growth potential of an already existing business, and for benchmarking it against global competition. A unique aspect of the Constraint Analysis is that it separates the "Intrinsic Business Attractiveness" factors from the management or "Fit Factors." The first set assesses the degree of knowledge-intensive, high value-added, strongly-proprietary content involved, and the second set evaluates the in-house competence to manage and fund the business. Intrinsic factors cannot be modified much, but weaknesses in the Fit Factor set can be strengthened through strategic alliances.

Also, this methodology when coupled with "Sensitivity Analysis" in a graphic format, can further reduce the risks involved, by quantifying those areas of further development which would have the greatest payoffs, if successful. It used a discounted cash flow return on investment (DCF-ROI), as a yardstick, in which all direct and indirect costs, as well as price and volume factors, are individually varied plus or minus 30% or more, to see what effect they would have on the DCF-ROI. This methodology also defines the limits of an envelope of further improvements that might possibly be achieved. To the degree that such improvements can be obtained (reduced costs, increased volume per unit of capital invested etc.), the Constraint Analysis score also would be improved.

In this context, the DCF-ROI becomes a measure of productivity which includes not only all direct and indirect costs, but also is an index of performance --- as reflected both in the marketplace price which a consumer is willing to pay, and in the P/E ratio of the company stock in the marketplace.

The Constraint Analysis involves 12 factors which have been identified through regression analysis to be especially important for achieving commercial success. They are divided into two groups of six each, one of which measures the intrinsic degree of 'knowledge-intensive, high value-added, proprietary" content of either an existing business, or a new opportunity. The second quantifies the degree to which necessary operating and management conditions currently exist (in house) to develop, scale-up, commercialize, and/or grow a business, the "Fit Factors."

Each of the 12 factors is scored on a scale of 0 to 10, and if the sum of the scores for all factors is 80 points or more (out of a possible 120) the probability of success for a new venture is 80% to 90%. Such a score also defines an existing business as a growth business. Below 80 points, the probability of success (as defined in Figure 13) falls off very rapidly for a new venture. Existing businesses with scores between 60 and 80 points indicate limited, if any, sustainable growth potential, but continued operation as a "cash cow" can be justified. Below 60 points, additional investments are unwise, and the business should be "harvested" for cash, or divested. Scoring an already existing business in this fashion helps to benchmark it against competition. Even more importantly, it allows different types of businesses, or investment opportunities to be compared against each other for an always limited supply of capital. A decision tree results (Figure 14).

Criteria for Commercial Success

o   A Going Concern
o   Planning Expansion
o   Sales Growth on Plan
o   Profits Exceed Plan
o   Positive After Tax Profits
o   Cumulative Positive Cash Flow
o   Invisible Assets Increasing in Value
o   Positive Company Support

Figure 13

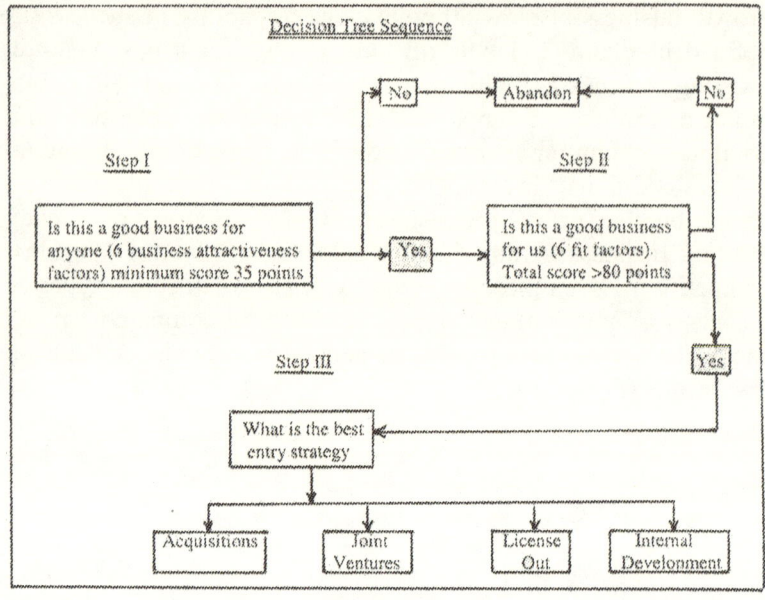

Figure 14

The score for Intrinsic Business Attractiveness factors (Step I), should be at least 35 points before proceeding to Step II; and a total score of 80 points or more is needed for serious further consideration. However, if Step I is satisfied, but Step II is weak, then the missing "Fit Factors" might still be acquired through various forms of strategic alliances. A new venture to be successful, should have 5 to 10 times better cost/performance than existing products or processes already in the marketplace --- and this usually correlates with scores over 80 points. However, it is therefore important to determine the actual performance/cost specifications, that will be needed to achieve a 5 to 10 times competitive advantage, and then to realistically assess the likelihood of realizing those specifications.

- High temperature superconductivity (HTS) wires can carry electricity with almost no losses over long distances. In principle, this technology could revolutionize the utility industry --- bringing remote sources of wind, solar, geothermal, hydroelectric, and tidal energy to industrialized areas, while tying the continental grid together in a seamless power distribution network. Present (HTS) technology can carry about 40,000 amps/cm^2 of current, sufficient for some specialty requirements. But current capacity over 100,000 amps/cm^2 will be needed to begin to justify long distance cables. Over 1 million amps/cm^2 have been demonstrated in 1 centimeter lengths, but these are far from commercial operation. The intrinsic business attractiveness for HTS cables and other applications is extraordinary, but no company alone, has been able to justify the cost and risk, of further developments. Therefore, the Department of Energy, in a landmark model of collaboration, has catalyzed the formation of several industry-managed, vertically-integrated consortia (for motors, generators, fault current limiters, (as well as transmission lines) and is partially subsidizing through seed funding, the first and second stages of development. None of the companies currently involved have the resources to undertake these developments alone.

The Six Business Attractiveness Factors

Six factors have been identified as useful in determining the degree of knowledge- intensive, high value-added, proprietary content of a new opportunity, sufficient in degree to justify significant investment of time and resources (Figure 15).

o   Sales, Profit Potential

(Score a maximum of 5 points for the sales potential, and 5 points maximum for the profit potential.)

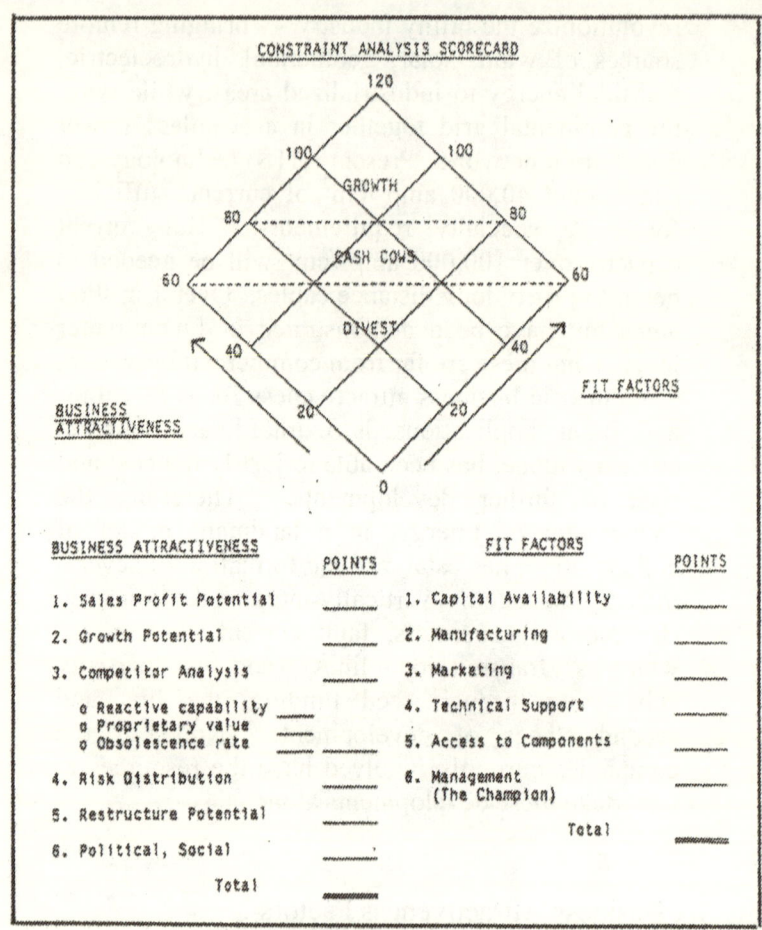

Figure 15

For Sales: The question is, will this opportunity, if successful, make a significant contribution to current sales? A company with $100 million in sales might find a $10-15 million contribution attractive. However, a company with $1 billion in sales, might want the new opportunity to be able to contribute at least $100 million in sales. Moreover, the importance of both sales volume and profitability are not linear, but exponential functions (Figure 16).

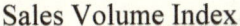
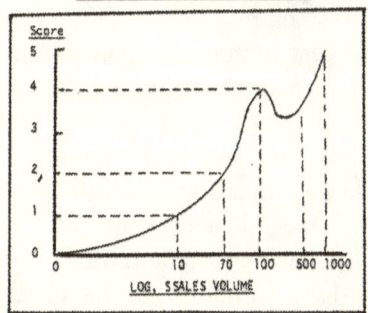
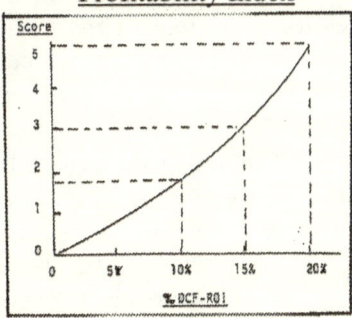

Figure 16

The sales volume index rises exponentially to about $100 million a year, but then dips, because what has been a niche market for large companies, somewhat protected from visibility, then begins to be much more attractive. Moreover, as the market continues to expand, multiple smaller segments involving additional service and other applications usually emerge, adding value to the total business, and accelerating its expansion and attractiveness.

For Profits, the question is: can this opportunity provide 10% or higher after tax profits, and a return on equity over 20% (5 points). Sales volume without profitability is the definition of a commodity business, which may not survive long in a hyper-competitive global marketplace (now awash in excess capacity). A discounted cash flow return on investment (DCF-ROI) provides a reasonable measure of potential profitability, since it can correct for inflation and also discounts for alternative risk-free investments, such as Government securities. A DCF-ROI of 20% or higher would rate a score of 5 points, and the sum of both the sales and profits scores, provides the total score for this Intrinsic Business Attractiveness factor.

o   Growth Potential (Score on a scale of 0 to 10)

"A rising tide raises all the boats, even the leaky ones." Therefore, the rate of market growth, or the ability to rapidly penetrate an existing market, can be very important for increased economies of scale, reduced costs and growing profits.

- The transistor not only obsoleted a slow-growing vacuum tube amplifier Market, but also exploded this market by enabling the development of hundreds of niche applications, which vacuum tubes could not begin to serve. Many entrepreneurs have ridden this rising tide.

Moreover, the "first-mover" of an innovation in a rapidly growing market has a critical opportunity to get down the learning curve (Figure 17) and establish a dominant design. On average, every doubling of volume in an industry results in 20% or greater reduced costs. Competitors 1 and 2 then are left behind, as the innovator moves from 3 to 4, but maintains the price just below competitors costs (strategic pricing). This also establishes a "dominant design" against which competitors must attempt improvements but without the same economies of scale.

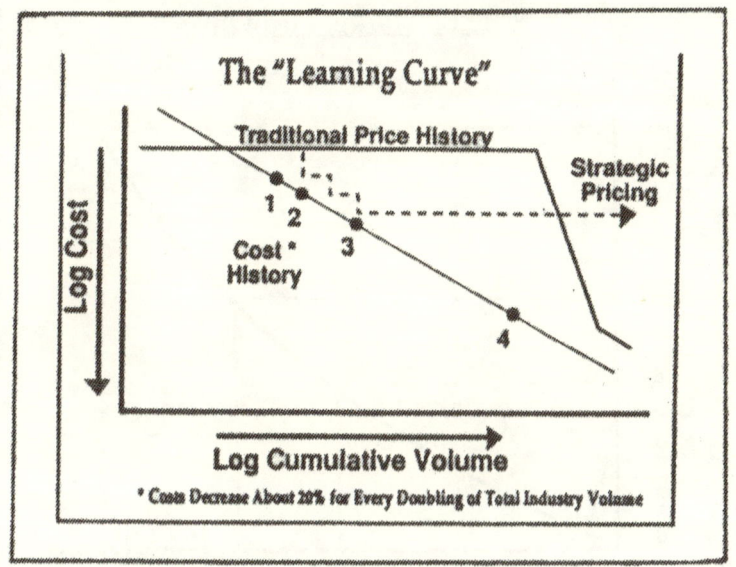

Figure 17

o Microsoft has established a dominant design for personal computers with 90% of the market using "windows" technology. Creative uses of the Internet eventually may by-pass the need for "Windows," but profits generated by Windows software should sustain high levels of continued innovation by Microsoft, in other rapidly growing markets.

In the past, companies such as Timex, Xerox, Kodak and IBM have established dominant positions, and prospered for a time, but failed to take advantage of newer technology serving a growing need. For this factor, score 10 points for market growth in excess of 20% per year, and lesser points as shown in Figure 18.

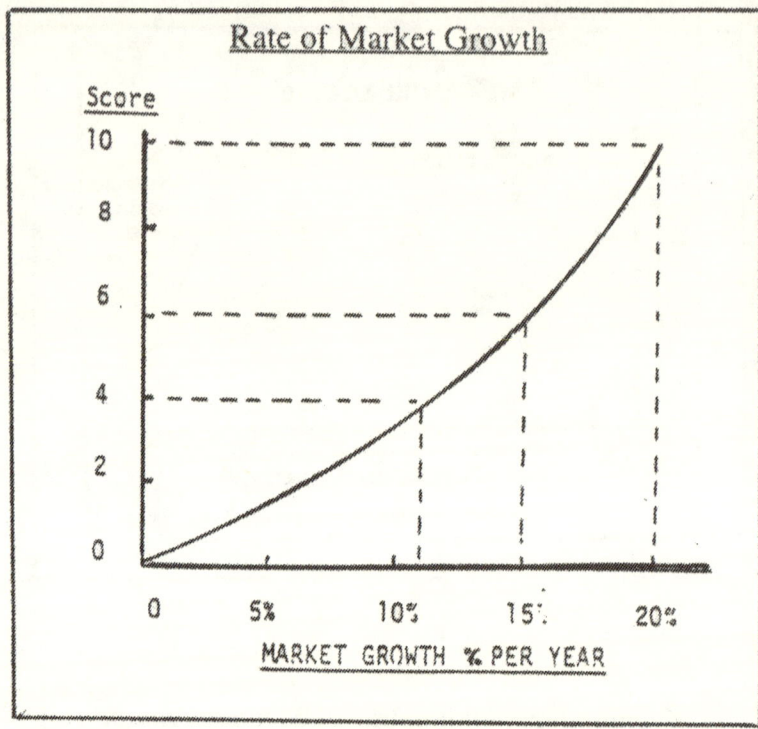

Figure 18

o   The Competitive Environment Factor

There are several important facets of the competitive environment that need to be assessed. One of these involves the ability of a large competitor with deep pockets to react effectively to loss of market share and profitability. A second involves the degree of patent or copyright protection which can insulate an innovation from competition; and a third involves the rate of technology-driven obsolescence of the business involved.

A large entrenched competitor operating obsolescent technology, nevertheless can react by lowering prices (at the expense of running a negative cash flow, to buy time) with the hope of being a fast-follower, and then later overwhelming the innovator with superior marketing, distribution, production, and access to capital. (However, this may not be possible if penetration by the new entrant is too rapid.)

In the past, a product or process has passed through 4 stages in its life cycle, as shown in Figure 19. Following the appearance of an innovation, a number of fast-followers begin to enter the market with variations and improvements, and this ushers in a second stage of dynamic development. Eventually in stage III, a dominant design appears which then freezes out further radical changes, and the market begins to consolidate to a few large companies.

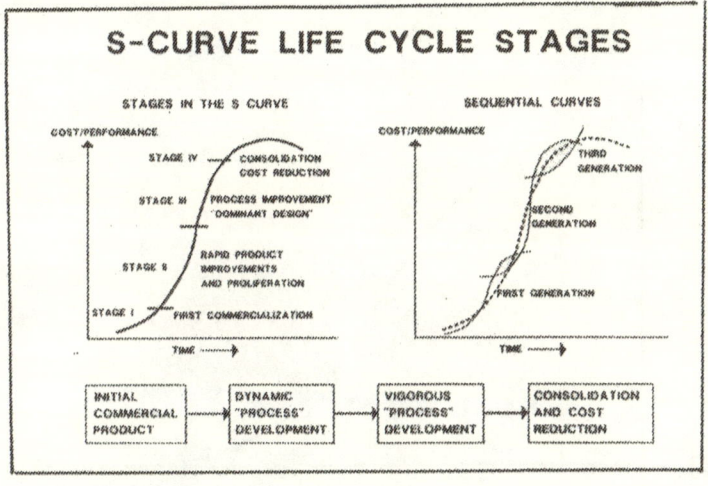

Figure 19

o The Betamax video recorder may have been technically superior to the VHS, but lost out when the VHS marketing strategy captured a dominant share of the market and the accompanying economies of scale.

Finally, in stage IV, the market has developed, profitability has eroded --- and a next-generation system may be appearing. However, with collapsing life cycles, many innovations may never see the third and fourth stages, mitigating the fast-follower strategy. Nevertheless, competitor reactivity cannot be underestimated. Therefore, rate this factor on a scale of 0 to 4, with the highest score for a badly fragmented market involving only small competitors, and a low score for a market dominated by a "gorilla". (Intel has about 80% of the microprocessor business and Microsoft about 90% of the PC software business.) (Figure 20)

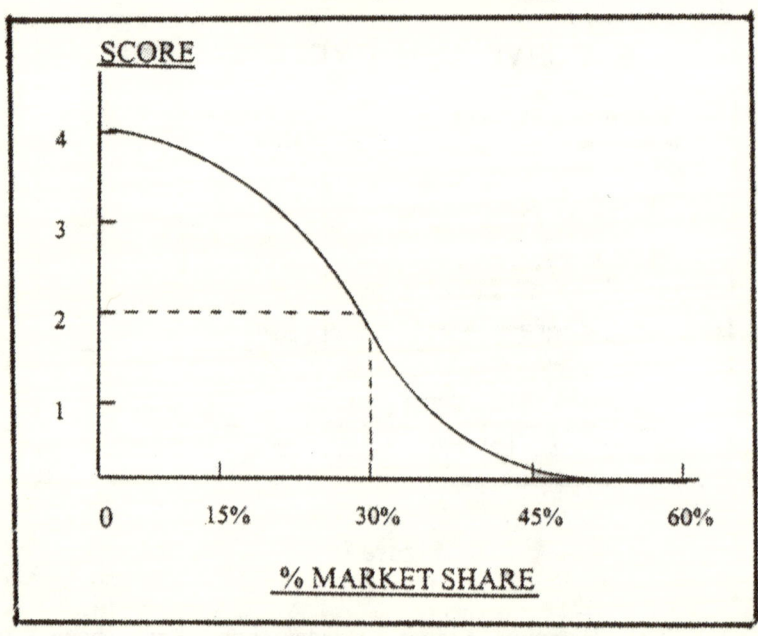

Figure 20

The degree of proprietary patent or copyright protection (score on a scale of 0 to 3) is the second consideration in assessing the competitive environment. A patent or copyright provides a constitutional right to a legal monopoly for an innovation (Figure 21). A basic composition of matter patent provides the strongest protection. Pharmaceuticals, specialty chemicals, and advanced materials often are based on such patents. However, a basic patent can be substantially further strengthened by process or construction (support) patents, and by use or application (picket) patents. Worldwide coverage in the most important countries is expensive but necessary for any significant development. Picket patents usually need to be filed in only one country, essentially to block competitors from filing disclosures, and blocking use of the technology in limited areas.

Degree of Proprietary Protection

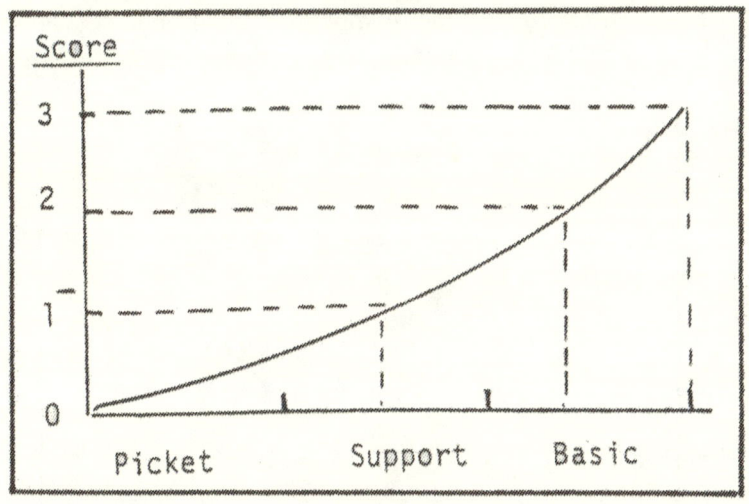

Figure 21

Technological obsolescence is the third consideration in assessing the competitive environment (score on a scale of 0 to 3). Many patents may never see a full 17 year life, before they are obsoleted by newer technology. However, with continued innovative development a basic patent life can often be extended by "continuations in part," based on the original date of the discovery (which should be witnessed). However, early obsolescence is a growing concern, and the expected life cycle is an important consideration (Figure 22). Score on a scale of 0 to 3.

An important advance in an area of low technical activity involving small competitors, would rate the highest score. An area of very high technical activity involving large highly competent competitors would rate a low score. Moreover, in such an area of high activity, immediate access to production, marketing and distribution and early market entry would be important. Licensing or joint venture strategies can accelerate market entry and reduce this risk. The sum of these three factors: (1) competitor reactivity, (2) the degree of proprietary protection, and (3) the rate of technological obsolescence, can provide an effective assessment of the competitive environment within which a business must operate.

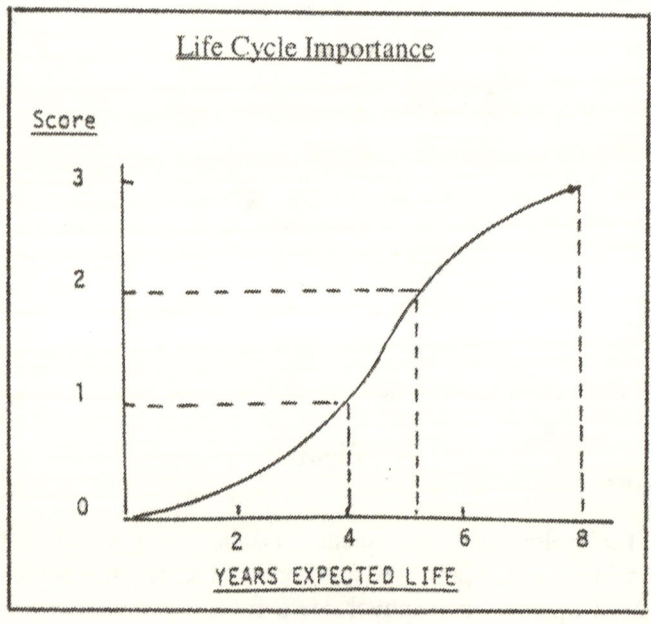

Figure 22

- Risk Distribution Factor (Score on a scale of 0 to 10)

Any business that has "all its eggs in one basket" can be more vulnerable to a superior innovation in its area of operation, than one which has spread the risk of obsolescence over a diversity of market areas, each with their own proprietary character (Figure 23).

- Timex, after World War II, turned its precision tooling expertise (developed during the War for making fuses) to mass production of a watch which was shockproof, waterproof, had a sweep second hand, used a newly developed hard material (Armaloy) in place of jewels, and cost less than $10.00. Timex then captured about 50% of the world watch market by the early 1960's. But they failed to appreciate the quartz watch innovation with its few moving parts, that didn't fit the Timex "core competency" --- and lost the market to Japanese companies.

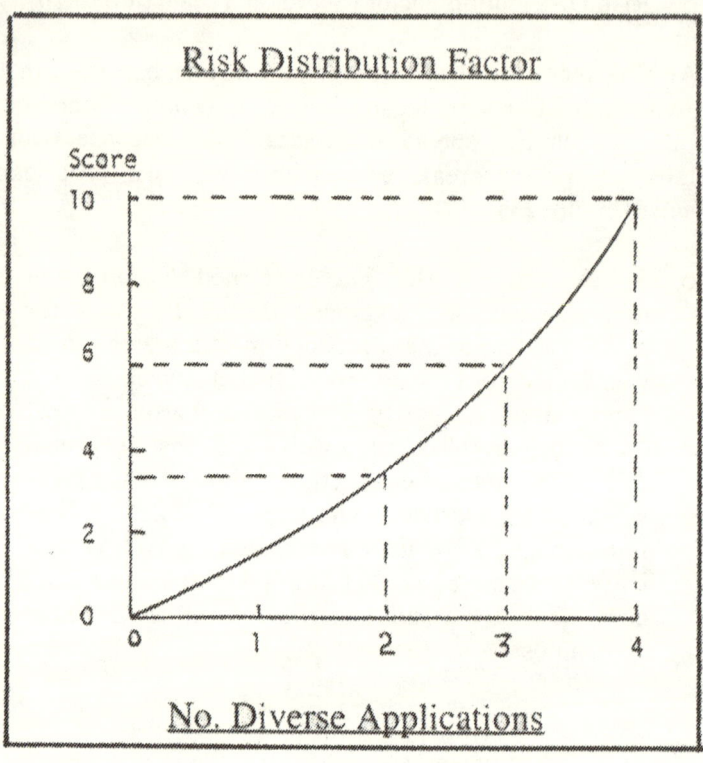

Figure 23

Therefore, it is important that a common platform and core competency have a diversity of end uses, each with individual proprietary character sufficient to insulate the company from a surprise innovation which may threaten one but not all of them. Different marketing and distribution requirements involved for each segment can be satisfied through strategic alliances, for accelerated market entry.

- o Opportunity to Restructure an Industry (Score on a scale of 0 to 10)

A cost/benefit improvement of 5 to 10 times over existing technology usually is required to restructure an industry. Incremental improvements cannot do this, but the current proliferation of basic discoveries and the emergence of several dozen "critical technologies" likely will restructure most industries over the next decade or two. The value of such a breakthrough is enormous for a first-mover, and can be significant for niche market followers. Such a development can be leveraged to the degree that it enables different applications to achieve superior performance.

- o A major advance in electrical energy storage has provided 100 times greater power density than is available from current batteries, and 30 to 50 times greater energy storage than conventional capacitors. In combination with conventional batteries for pulse power applications, it not only provides much better performance, but also extends the backup battery life by 3 to 5 times, depending upon the duty cycle.

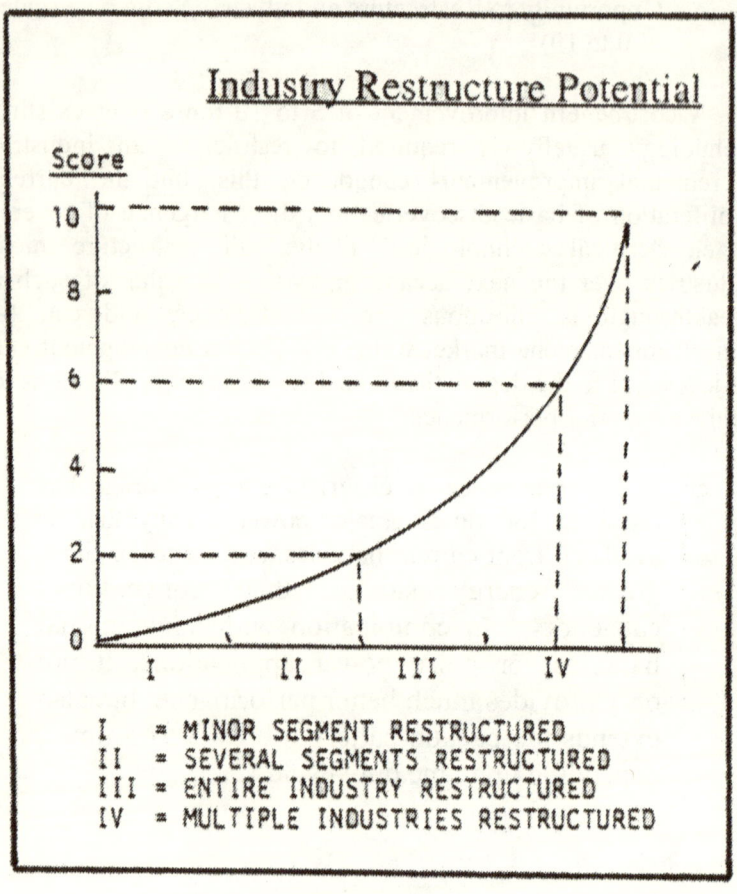

Figure 24

As an enabling component, it is being broadly licensed for use in cellular telephony, defibrillators, power tools, fork lift trucks, uninterruptible power supplies, and many other applications. However, a development of this magnitude can be further leveraged through joint ventures in which equity participation provides a downstream multiplier of the return on investment from other licensing or internal development of end uses alone.

All possibilities for leveraging may not be recognized at first. Therefore, a systematic market search can be important, first to identify possible applications, and secondly to prioritize them for first market entry. (Score according to Figure 24).

- o Political and Social Constraints (Score on a scale of 0 to 10)

All governments intervene in the marketplace in myriad ways. These interventions include tariffs, quotas, product specifications, building and construction codes, emission levels for carbon dioxide, nitrogen oxides and other pollutants, as well as standards for the sale of securities and for broadcast and communications operations. In the U.S., liability laws currently result in industry payments over $200 billion per year, resulting from class action and other forms of punitive litigation. Dozens of local codes and restrictions must be complied with, which add costs and time delays and can seriously reduce the attractiveness of an opportunity.

Finally, an incoherent combination of monetary, fiscal and regulatory policies, exacerbated be fluctuating exchange rates, can radically change the environment for sustained investments needed for survival. In the U.S., Federal Reserve initiated boom and bust cycles (resulting from manipulation of interest rates and the money supply) have introduced periods of uncertainty for investment, that have been destructive --- but must be anticipated by management strategies. Unfortunately, the multiplicity and variety of these "exogenous" interventions, makes them difficult to quantify. Also, certain types of businesses are more sensitive to some types of political and social intervention than are others:

- o Import-export businesses are especially sensitive to exchange rate changes, pharmaceuticals to FDA regulations, automobiles to global warming legislation, and construction to endangered species concerns.

However, restrictive legislation for one industry may also create incentives for another. Score this factor with a neutral situation (neither restrictions or incentives) rated at 5 points; and with higher ratings if incentives are present, or lower ratings if there are negative factors (Figure 25). If an activity is either illegal or unethical, the rating is not only zero, but requires abandonment of the program.

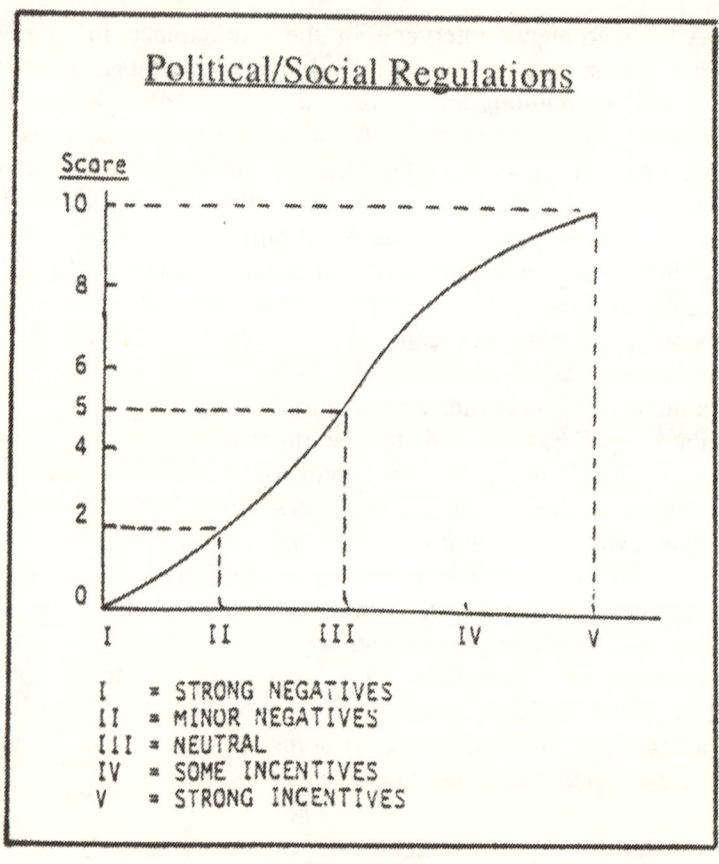

Figure 25

Six Business "Fit" Factors

Because they are intrinsic, the Business "Attractiveness" Factors are not easily modified, and their total score should be at least 35 points to seriously consider the "Fit Factors." Assuming that the program under consideration is <u>not</u> illegal or unethical, and that the total score for Business Attractiveness is at least 35 points, then the Fit Factors can be quantified.

o   <u>Capital Availability</u> (Score on a scale of 0 to 10)

A discounted cash flow return on investment (DCF-ROI) of 20% establishes a high hurdle rate for availability of capital. Large companies with heavy cash flows might choose to ignore this hurdle, but this is not advisable. Also, an undercapitalized company may not have access to funds at any rate. For start-up businesses, lack of capital usually results in major dilutions of equity for the entrepreneurs involved, as a result of multiple rounds of financing. Cash rescue in periods of distress also usually results in loss of management control. Therefore, affordable levels of capital must be available as needed from a combination of equity and debt financing. Also, once commercial operation begins, the generation of sustained cash flow should be sufficient to finance further measured growth (hedged for negative surprises), or at least sufficient to create options for additional leverage.

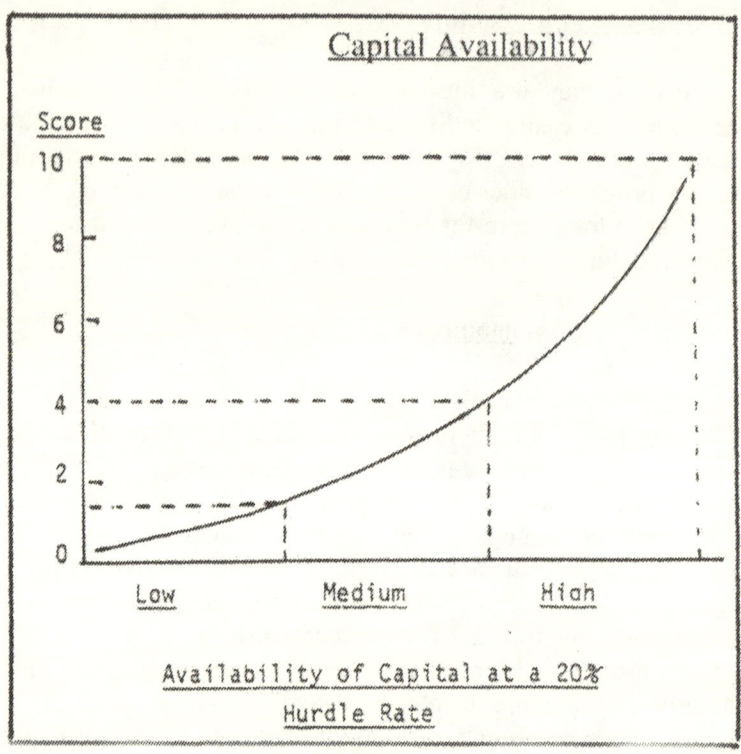

Figure 26

Capital needs usually are underestimated by a factor of at least two, and negative surprise factors can multiply the requirements. Therefore, contingency plans for rapid reduction of overhead and other direct costs should be worked out in advance. The rule of thumb is that cash flow requirements for manufacturing, marketing, and distribution can exceed the cost of initial development by a factor of 10. Services, software, and light manufacturing businesses tend to be less capital-intensive, and shared, flexible computer-integrated manufacturing (FCIM) facilities, now being developed, can mitigate some of the initial entry costs and accelerate prototyping. Dedicated facilities making a single product often can be obsolete before repayment of their investment.

In the United States, the cost of capital has averaged 5 to 7 times greater than in Japan and other countries. Incoherent fiscal and monetary policies largely have been responsible. As a result, the hurdle rate for risk investments has been so high for venture capitalists, that when investing in opportunities still in development, they require large proportions of the equity.

Other limited sources of capital have included small business innovation research (SBIR) grants from U.S. government laboratories, which provide $75,000 Phase I grants and $750,000 Phase II grants. However, only about one in 100 applications are funded. The Commerce Department's advanced technology program (ATP) has a growing budget, but one which also does not meet the demand. Finally, the Defense Advanced Research Projects Agency (DARPA) funds promising dual-use developments that have both military and commercial potential. Friends and individual investors can be another limited source of funds. However, reliance on such funding is not advisable, and the time-critical availability of funding is an important constraint. Score as illustrated in Figure 26

- o Marketing and Distribution Requirements (Score on a scale of 0 to 10)

Early entry and rapid penetration of global markets is critical in maximizing the return on any investment. Moreover, time-critical access to global markets often will require formation of strategic alliances. "It is better to have 50% of something than 100% of nothing." Alliances must be properly structured and the individuals involved must have strong incentives to produce results. Separate arrangements may be required for different market segments, but the degree of differences in needed skills and capabilities can provide both risk distribution and barriers to entry for competitors.

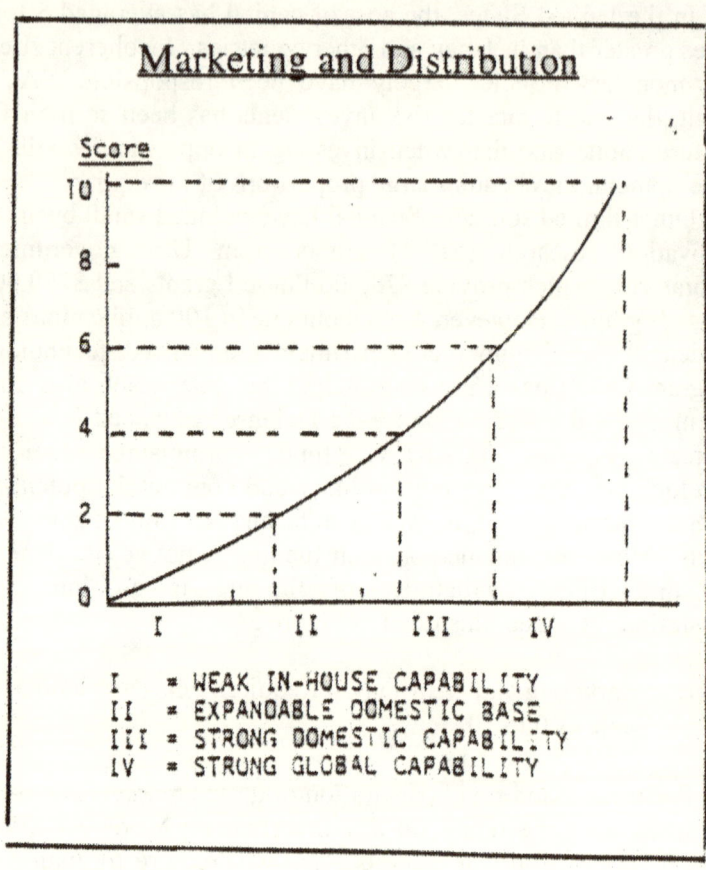

Figure 27

The U.S. Department of Commerce has set up a number of joint venture arrangements with developing countries to facilitate formation of alliances. Contacts can be made through the Office of Technology Administration and through foreign commercial officers at many U.S. embassies. Score this factor as illustrated in Figure 27.

o <u>Manufacturing Capabilities</u> (Score on a scale of 0 to 10)

This factor is measured in terms of the ability to rapidly prototype a new development and provide early market entry with sustainable, reproducible precision production. Elements involved include bench scale and pilot plant facilities that are flexible and computer-integrated and can provide interim production at reasonable costs while gauging the need for rate of capacity increases. FCIM modules are now being developed that can be share-owned and time critically accessed for rapid prototyping and early market entry. These modules involve metal machining, plastics forming and molding, ceramics processing, and Mechano-electronic assembly systems. Effective use of these facilities requires designing for production at the earliest stages of development.

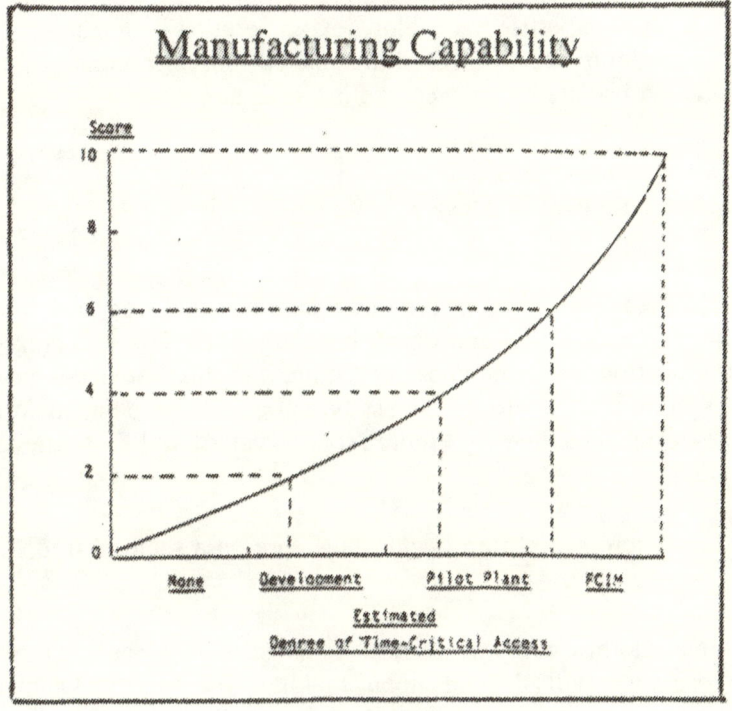

Figure 28

Opportunities that do not require sophisticated production capabilities, such as software and many services, automatically rate scores of 10. For others, score as illustrated in Figure 28.

- Technology Support Function (Score on a scale of 0 to 10)

Rapidly advancing technology is now the primary engine driving all economies. Therefore, an effective technical competence increasingly will be essential for industrial competitiveness. This function involves a number of important capabilities, including:

1. A strong sales service function
2. An ability to make continuous incremental improvements in existing operations
3. The expertise to develop next-generation systems, deliberately designed to make current operations obsolete before a competitor does so

- Technical Services to Sales (Score on a scale of 0 to 3)

Support of sales in the field can be vital for sustained customer satisfaction and repeat business. This is a specialized skill function, but often does not require a sophisticated technical background. Therefore, it must be supported on demand in a time-critical fashion by more sophisticated skills whenever needed.

- Incremental Improvements (Score on a scale of 0 to 4)

Near-term competitiveness and sustained cash flows increasingly will depend upon making 5% to 10% annual improvements in cost/performance for most businesses. This process requires concurrent engineering skills needed from the laboratory bench to commercial demonstration. In addition, it requires a professionally staffed computer-aided literature search function because important developments can surface anywhere. "A good idea doesn't care who has it." This very important world-scan capability must be designed to identify both new discoveries that might synergize with existing operations, as well a to provide early warning of next-generation developments that might make existing systems obsolete.

- Next-Generation Systems (Score on a scale of 0 to 3)

The United States currently spends some $35 billion each year for basic research. The United Kingdom is next with about 10% of that amount. All other nations spend less. Moreover, it is this unique (and unmatchable) capability that now generates most of the Nobel Prizes and has produced about two dozen critical technologies that will restructure almost every industry over the next two decades and dominate the 21st century. From now on, no U.S. or other industrial nation company can expect to maintain profitability in any commodity business unless it is protected by quotas or tariffs. Survival will depend upon making significant investments in these next-generation technologies with the deliberate intent to make current operations obsolete as soon as possible.

This requires a high level and broad spectrum of technical capabilities that few companies alone can hold captive. Yet survival in the longer term depends upon the ability to access such capabilities. Often, this will require collaboration in vertically integrated consortia -- a management style not easily accepted by a fiercely independent corporate culture.

The sum of these scores constitutes the figure of merit for this technical support capability (Figure 29).

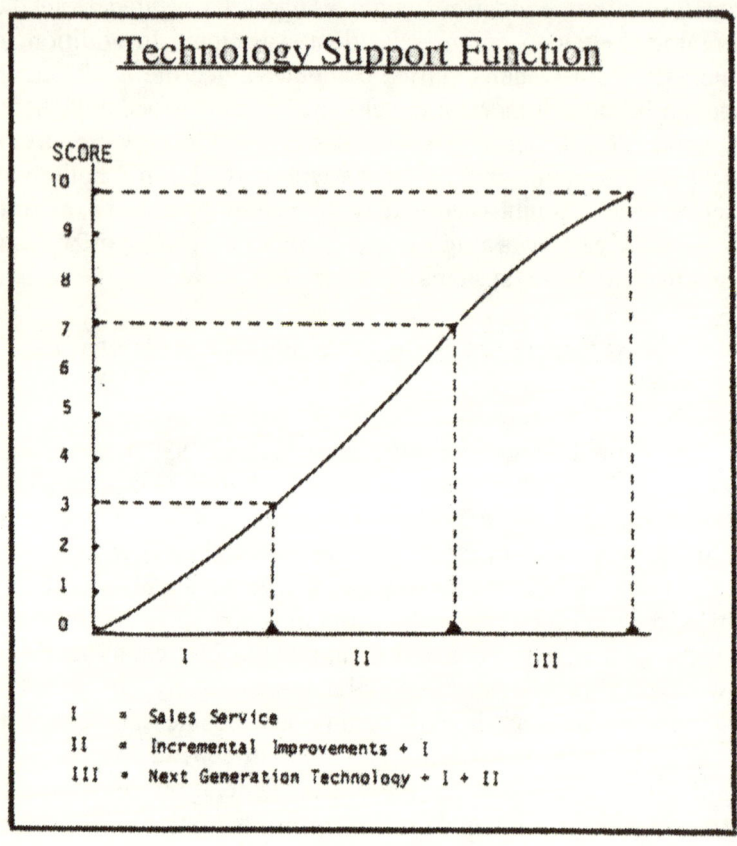

Figure 29

o Access to Critical Materials and Components (Score on a scale of 0 to 10)

A time-critical, assured supply of raw materials or components is essential for sustained profitable operation. Even a temporary shortage or interruption of a vital intermediate raw material, an essential microchip, a circuit board, or a testing service can push a small business into Chapter 11, or make a larger company vulnerable to takeover if its stock price falls below book value. Dependency upon imports from politically unstable countries is unwise, and contingency plans that include reserve supplies are important. Sole source procurement also can result in shrinking profit margins as the supplier takes advantage of the control possessed to raise prices. Rate the sensitivity to disruption as illustrated (Figure 30).

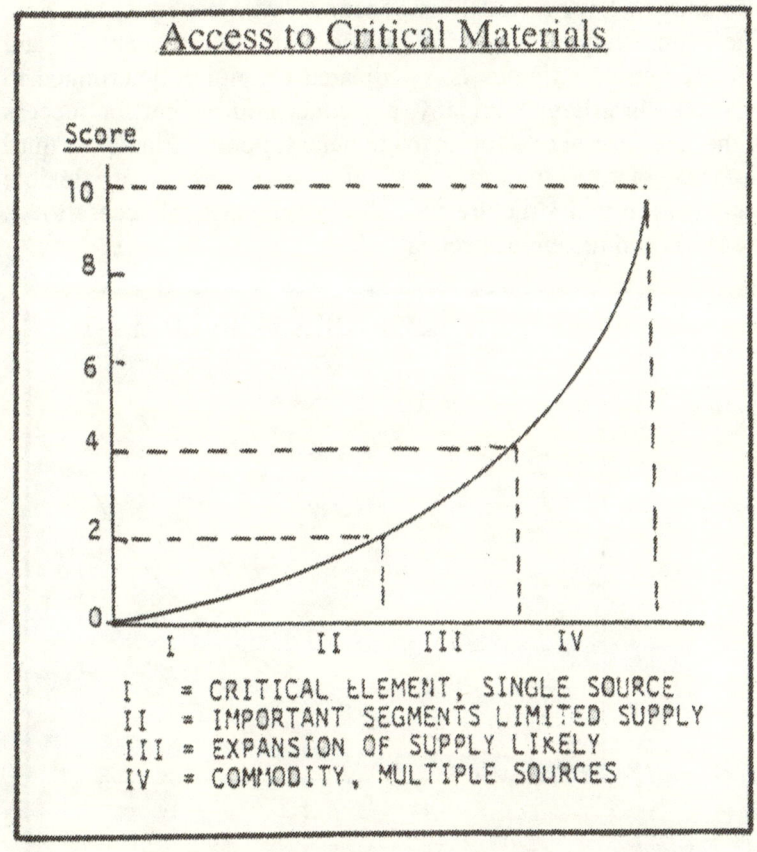

Figure 30

o   Management Competence (Score 0 to 10)

Hernando deSoto, a Peruvian, has written a book based on a 7-year study of Latin American companies, in which he points out that the definition of an underdeveloped country is one where the entrepreneurial function has been made illegal. This is true, of course, of all the Marxist-Socialist economies, but it is also true in part in many large companies where bureaucratic layers of managers have seriously impeded the intrapreneurial function. The first requirement for successful entrepreneurial and intrapreneurial activities is a dedicated champion determined to succeed. In a large company, a second requirement for success is the need for active top management support. Finally, a third element that is required for all operations is a flexible organization and structure that allows time-critical access to all the skills and resources needed.

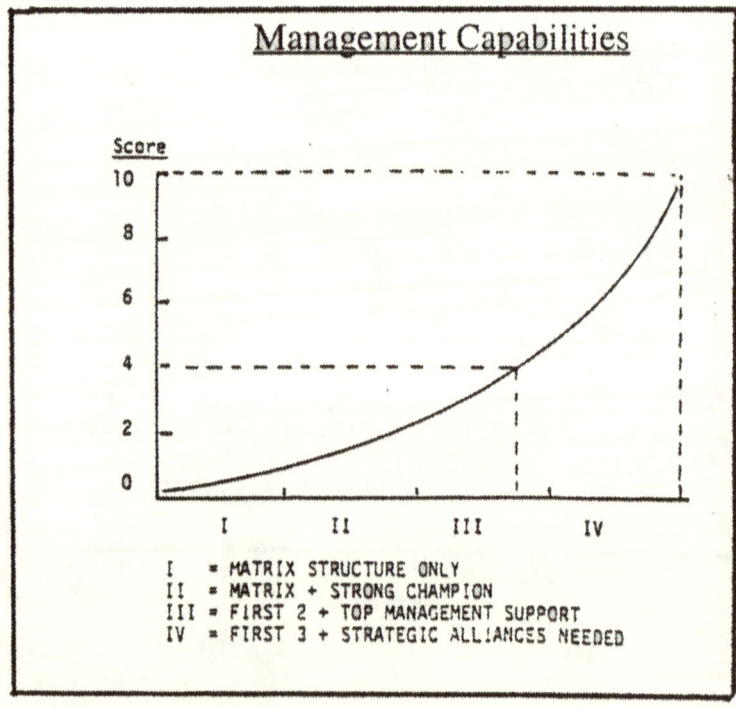

Figure 31

The champion must be technically competent and have management experience. High levels of energy, good communication skills, the ability to relate easily to all types of people, and enormous persistence also are needed.

Top management commitment means intervention at all levels of the organization to ensure that skills and resources of the organization are available when needed, and that the fledgling innovation is protected from existing entrenched profit centers that are competing for the same resources.

A concurrent engineering (task force) or matrix form of organization is essential to allow time-critical access to needed skills and resources. Increasingly, various forms of strategic alliance structures also will be required to pool skills and resources, share risk, and accelerate development times for early commercialization and an all-important first-mover advantage. The limited partnership structure is particularly useful for both funding and managing a major innovation which may be beyond the skill capabilities and risk threshold for an individual company. Score this factor as illustrated in Figure 31.

o   Regression Analysis Data

Figure 32 (next page) tabulates several dozen projects, some of which in retrospect should never have been undertaken, and others that resulted in varying degrees of success as measured by a discounted cash flow return on investment. Regression analysis produced a correlation factor (r) of 0.924, with a coefficient of determination of 0.853, and the coefficient of non-determination of 0.147 (3). The T value (14.451) also is very high, indicating that the possibility of zero correlation within the population is unlikely (less than 5%) and that a 95% confidence exists for the correlations postulated.

Figure 33 plots the correlation between % ROI and the constraint scores. Return on investment rises exponentially with the constraint score. The author was intimately involved in these projects over several decades, commencing in an earlier, "more naive" time. Committing the time, energy, and enthusiasm of a young researcher to projects that have minimal hope of commercial success can be dispiriting and was the origin of the constraint analysis. The analysis developed over a number of years, and much better results were obtained as the opportunity for management control over investment opportunities occurred.

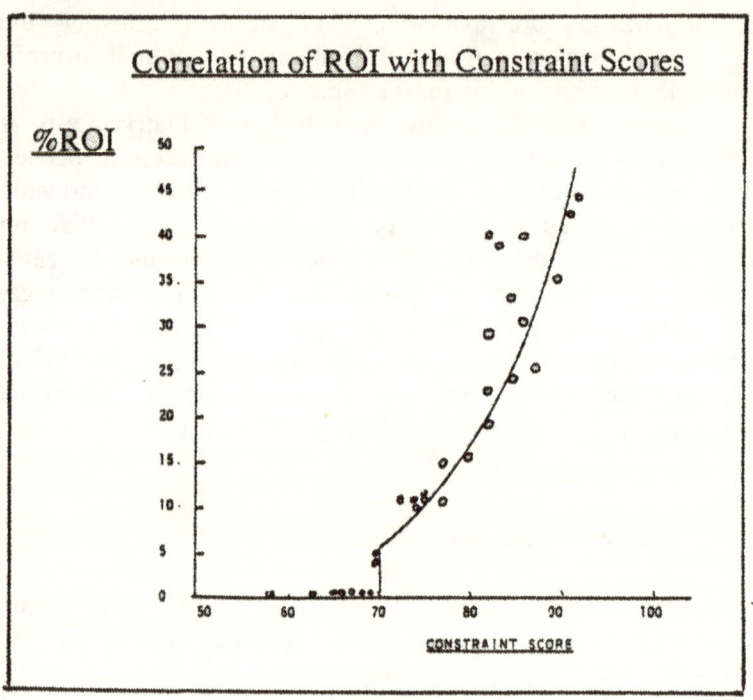

Figure 32

The analysis was picked up by T.Ohe (7) in Japan, when resident at the Wharton School of Business. He carried out a study of some 38 corporate diversification ventures involving 18 major Japanese corporations. In this study, 80% of the ventures were manufacturing and 20% were service businesses. Regression analysis showed a strong correlation with the fit factors and 4 of the 6 business attractiveness factors (Figure 34).

Lack of correlation with factors 5 and 6 in the business attractiveness category and with the need for patent protection reflects the fact that the projects selected were not based on new R&D but were diversifications into existing businesses with limited proprietary character. Also, the regulatory climate in Japan has been more benign than in the United States (80,000 new U.S. regulations were legislated between 1980 and 1990). The study was undertaken because the active diversification efforts by large companies in Japan had met with limited success (5). Those that were successful generally had constraint scores of 80 points or more (Figure 35).

Project Analysis

Project	Business Attractiveness							Fit Factors						Results	
	1	2	3	4	5	6	(TOT)	1	2	3	4	5	6	(TOT)	Sum	% ROI
Specialty Polymer	5	5	4	2	0	5	(21)	8	3	4	7	9	5	(36)	57	0%
Ore Flotation Agent	5	5	3	3	0	5	(21)	9	8	2	9	10	4	(42)	63	0%
Rocket Fuel	7	5	2	1	4	6	(25)	7	7	2	9	10	5	(40)	65	0%
Specialty Polyester	7	7	5	4	0	5	(28)	8	7	8	8	0	7	(38)	66	0%
Zinc/Chloride Battery	5	5	2	5	5	5	(27)	4	4	3	7	10	5	(33)	60	0%
High Temp Polymer	7	5	4	6	0	5	(27)	6	5	5	7	10	6	(39)	66	0%
HF From Phosphates	6	5	5	7	0	7	(30)	5	7	4	6	10	5	(37)	67	0%
Vulcanization Agent	5	4	4	3	2	5	(23)	8	8	7	8	9	5	(45)	68	0%
Quiet Ride Tire	5	4	4	2	2	6	(23)	8	8	7	8	10	5	(46)	69	0%
Ziegler Catalyst	7	8	2	2	4	5	(28)	8	6	5	8	10	5	(42)	70	6%
Retort Pouch	8	5	3	4	4	6	(28)	7	7	7	6	10	6	(42)	70	4%
Synthetic Ethaverine	5	4	5	2	0	6	(22)	9	8	8	9	10	7	(51)	73	11%
Polystyrene Cup	7	6	3	7	0	6	(29)	6	5	7	8	10	7	(44)	73	12%
Specialty Phenolic	5	4	2	5	0	5	(21)	7	10	10	7	10	7	(51)	72	9%
Scale Inhibitor	5	6	3	3	0	5	(22)	9	8	9	9	10	5	(50)	72	12%
Emulsion Butadiene	8	6	4	3	3	5	(29)	7	9	7	8	10	5	(46)	75	13%
Phenolic Dye	5	4	7	4	2	5	(27)	8	9	9	7	10	5	(48)	75	12%
Chlorine Membrane Cell	7	6	4	3	5	5	(30)	8	7	8	7	10	7	(47)	77	15%
Edible Sausage Casing	8	8	4	4	5	7	(36)	8	4	7	5	10	7	(41)	77	16%
Barrier Plastic (CO)	8	7	5	7	3	5	(37)	7	6	5	8	10	6	(42)	77	11%
Fire Retardant	6	8	3	7	0	7	(31)	8	9	8	6	10	6	(47)	78	15%
Bipolar Chlorine Cell	6	6	8	4	3	5	(29)	8	9	9	8	10	7	(51)	80	16%
Instant Corrosion Meter	5	5	7	5	3	7	(32)	7	6	9	9	10	7	(50)	82	19%
Corrosion Inhibitor	8	6	5	7	2	6	(34)	8	8	9	9	5	9	(48)	82	29%
Specialty Emulsifier	6	8	7	8	6	7	(40)	7	9	4	8	9	5	(42)	82	21%
High Impact PVC	10	8	8	10	3	5	(42)	7	8	3	7	10	5	(40)	82	42%
Fine Particle PVC	8	7	7	7	1	5	(35)	8	9	5	9	10	7	(48)	83	39%
Zinc Cerrophos Corrosion	8	6	7	5	4	5	(35)	9	9	6	8	10	7	(49)	84	32%
Plastic Beverage Bottle	8	8	5	5	3	6	(35)	8	8	9	7	10	7	(49)	84	24%
Pour Point Depressant	8	8	5	5	3	7	(36)	9	8	7	9	10	6	(49)	85	24%
Dimension Stable Anode	9	8	5	4	6	6	(38)	9	8	6	9	10	6	(48)	86	32%
Synthetic Wax	9	7	6	5	3	5	(35)	9	8	7	9	10	7	(51)	86	42%
Rubber Accelerant	8	5	4	7	5	5	(35)	9	9	9	8	10	7	(52)	87	28%
Oil Field Bacteridstat	8	8	6	6	3	7	(36)	9	8	9	8	10	7	(51)	89	37%
Rubber Antidegradant	9	8	6	7	6	9	(45)	7	9	3	9	10	8	(46)	91	46%
High Impact Polystyrene	9	8	6	7	5	5	(40)	9	10	7	9	10	6	(51)	91	42%
Agriculture Herbicide	9	9	7	7	4	6	(42)	8	9	9	9	10	7	(52)	92	49%

Correlation of Constraint Score Sum With % ROI   0.924

Coefficient of Determination   0.853

Coefficient of Non-Determination   0.147

T Value   14.461

Correlation of ROI With
    Business Attractiveness   0.8
    Fit Factors   0.6

Figure 33

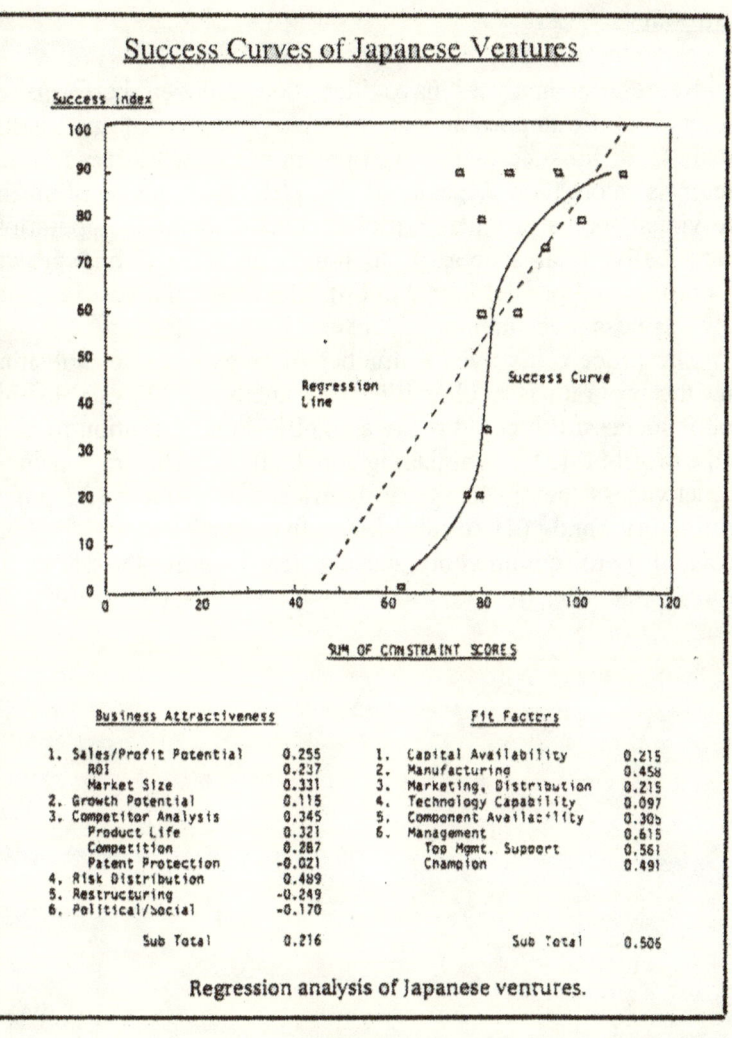

Figure 34

Summary

Regression analyses have identified a dozen performance factors that are important for profitable operation of an existing business, or for successful development of a new business. Each factor is scored on a scale of 0 to 10, and the sum of the individual scores provides a global benchmark of the operation. Statistically, total scores of 80 points or more define growth businesses and predict 8 or 9 out of 10 commercial successes for new business investments.

The process involves a number of steps: (1) establishing that the program is neither illegal or unethical; (2) establishing that if successful it could make a significant contribution to sales and profits; (3) establishing that the intrinsic business attractiveness factors justify a significant investment (35 points minimum); and (4) establishing that there exists a high probability of commercial success (total score 80 points or more).

References

1. D. B. Merrifield, "The Constraint Analysis for Assessment of Business Risks" <u>Technology Management</u> vol I, pp 42-53, (1994)

2. D. Bruce Merrifield, William M. Evan "The Department of Energy Superconductivity Initiative" <u>Research-Technology Management</u>, vol 41, No. 6 pp 44-48, (1998)

3. Bruce D. Henderson "Perspectives on Experience," The Boston Consulting Group (1968), Boston, Mass.

4. D. Bruce Merrifield, "Creative Destruction in the New Millenium" <u>Technology Management, Strategies and Applications</u> vol 3, pp 67-73, (1997)

5. R. N. Foster "Innovation, the Attacker's Advantage," <u>NY Summit Books</u> (1986)
   i. Also R. N. Becker, L. M. Speltz, "Putting the S-Curve to Work" <u>Research
   ii. Management</u> Sept/Oct (1983)

6. D. Bruce Merrifield, "Corporate Renewal Through Cooperation and Critical Technologies" <u>Research-Technology Management</u> July/August (1993) pp 14-18

7. Ohe, T. Honjos and Merrifield, D. B. "Japanese Corporate Ventures, Success Curve" <u>J. Business Venturing</u>, vol 7 #3 (1992) pp 171-180

KEY CONCEPTS TO REVIEW

- Statistically, why do so many new ventures never see the light of day?
- "On the back of an envelope" rate 2 or 3 companies, or profit center programs, with which you are familiar. Identify the one or two greatest weaknesses. What would you do about them?
- Where in the S-curve life cycle are these businesses, and what new technology could (or will) soon obsolete them. What advance would it take to have a 5 to 10 times cost/performance advantage over the existing systems/
- If you are currently employed by a company with two or more businesses, score each one, and plot the company profile on the constraint analysis scorecard. Are there any growth businesses (above 80 points), or "dogs" (below 60 points). What would you do with these businesses if you were the CEO?

CHAPTER IV

SENSITIVITY ANALYSIS

Perspective

The Constraint Analysis described in Chapter III, provides a powerful and effective methodology, both for screening new investment opportunities, and for benchmarking current business operations against global competition. In so doing, it also helps to identify the cost/performance operating specifications that must be achieved for the 5 to 10 times superiority, needed to capture market share in an already entrenched market.

However, a sensitivity analysis in a graphical format (Figure 35) can further quantify the relative contribution which each cost, volume and price factor makes to an "ROI-DCF* yardstick." This form of analysis also defines the "envelope of limits" for further improvements of each of these factors --- and therefore, can help focus ongoing development efforts. However, when the costs of making such further improvements becomes so great that they have little effect on the ROI-DCF, then the business has reached maturity, and probably should be "harvested" for cash or divested.

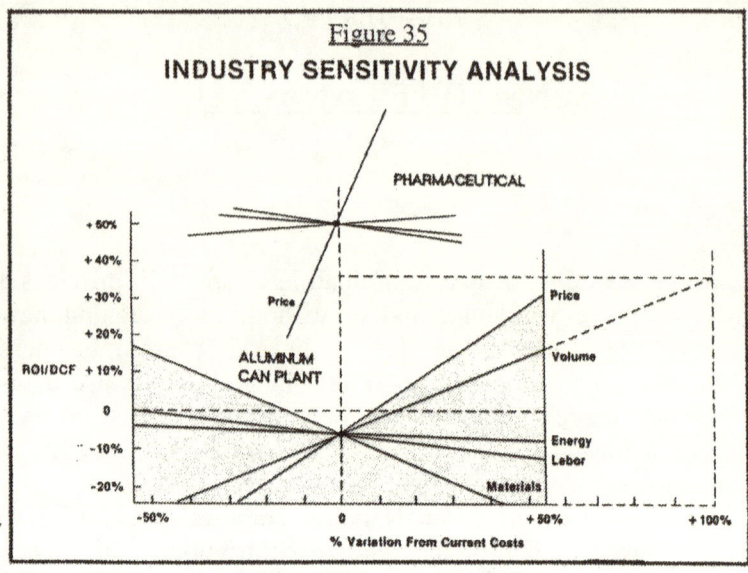

Figure 35

In this context, ROI-DCF yardsticks also become effective measures of productivity. Moreover, currently-used methods for measuring productivity are inaccurate. They compare price changes with labor-plus-capital costs --- and then make an "intuitive adjustment" for perceptions of "economic surplus" (added value in the form of better performance). But added-value comes in many forms that are difficult to quantify --- increased quality and uniformity, longer useful maintenance-free lives, greater reliability, safety, convenience and flexibility, user friendly --- as well as much superior performance (for example, the transistor vs. the vacuum tube, or a solution to life-threatening diseases, such as cancer, for which consumers would pay almost anything). Current productivity measurements do not and cannot, measure such varied forms of added value, which, however, are reflected in the ROI-DCF form of measurement.

In addition, the ROI-DCF quantifies the effects of dividend payout, debt, and inflation (a direct tax on equity), on the ability to retain earnings for further growth. The strategic importance of these factors is great.

The Sensitivity Analysis

The chart at the bottom of Figure 35, illustrates the sensitivity profile for an aluminum can plant, a low value-added business with excess capacity. This plant is running at a negative ROI-DCF of about 6%, but a price increase of 10% would result in breakeven. A 20% increase would result in a 5% ROI-DCF, but this is not feasible. Moreover, labor and energy costs account for only 3-4% each of total costs. Even a 50% decrease in either of these cost factors would barely reach breakeven --- although at that time, the company involved, was trying to cut union wages 10%!

In contrast, volume throughput is very sensitive, and doubling the number of cans per minute from 1000 to 2000 would be feasible, and would increase the DCF-ROI to 35%. However, this also would require a 20% increase in capital investments, and a 20% reduction of the DCF-ROI --- a net positive effect of 15%. However, the most sensitive cost factor is the cost of the aluminum, which accounts for about 70% of total costs. Using thinner can stock and necking-in the top of the can reduces this cost. Alternatively, use of plastics that have barrier properties to carbon dioxide would further reduce costs (beer is available now in plastic containers). However, there is little or no proprietary character to any of these improvements, and there are few barriers to entry for this commodity which is chronically in excess supply, so advantages of this sort would be short-lived.

By contrast, in the top half of Figure 35 is the profile of a highly proprietary pharmaceutical. Since this product is protected by strong composition of matter patents, and uniquely cures an important disease, it carries a high price relative to its cost, (the only game in town). The DCF-ROI is about 50% and sales are over $1 billion/year. When the patents eventually run out, or other competitive pharmaceuticals are developed, the price will fall rapidly and other cost factors will become more sensitive. But the "value-added" content involved is the important factor, determining the profitability.

A software program has been developed which prints out these sensitivity charts, and also runs out cash flow simulations for any selected set of assumptions, or periods of amortization. The sensitivity chart for a plastic bottle development program to replace metal cans for carbonated soft drinks is shown in Figure 36 (see also the detailed case history of this development at the end of this chapter). The example illustrates the importance of "unanticipated" factors that can intervene to upset the most carefully developed plans. In this case, the Continental Group, in which Continental Can was a division, was a secondary player, but came out the winner. Monsanto, the hands-down innovator, ended up writing off some $400 million in investments.

Continental unexpectedly acquired a first-mover advantage, which resulted in a spectacular 45% DCF-ROI for about two years, and this development initially captured about 70% of the plastic beverage bottle market for the one liter soft drink business in food stores. The first-mover advantage resulted when the FDA unexpectedly barred use of acrylonitril and polyvinyl chloride (PVC), (both superior materials) where competitors had focused their efforts.

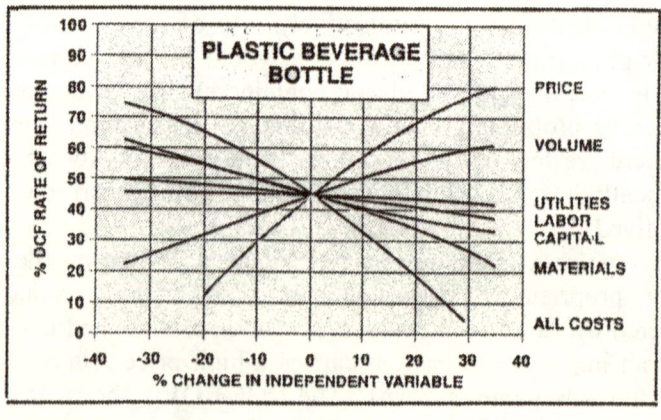

Figure 36

The winning company had hedged its bets, and also developed a bottle using a polyester material. When competitors finally began to enter, the business was divested, since no proprietary technology was involved, sufficient to protect the developments, (a poor initial decision that "lucked out").

This sensitivity model allows simulation of any number of assumptions. For example if a market price 10% below competition, but at a 20% DCF-ROI is selected, then the model can identify the mix of cost and volume parameters needed to achieve those conditions. If achieving those parameters is not technically feasible, the project should be reviewed. In this model, R&D costs can be expensed or capitalized.

Productivity Measurements

Current methods for measuring productivity do not and cannot adequately account for the added value (or "economic surplus") which now is the most important of the factors involved in measuring inflation. For example, a 1907 Ford would cost about $12,000 in current dollars, and the lowest cost Fords today would not be much more. But the value-added is enormous as reflected in performance, life, safety and convenience --- not measurable by the ratio of capital-plus-labor costs to price.

The Boskin study reports that inflation is probably overstated by at least 1% and the Nakamura study by over 2% (Figure 37). Nakamura's data indicate that productivity increases since 1975 have been 300% higher than reported, and average wage increases have increased 35% over this period instead of -9% as reported by Government data. Also the Gross Domestic Product (GDP) has been twice that reported. (Figure 37)

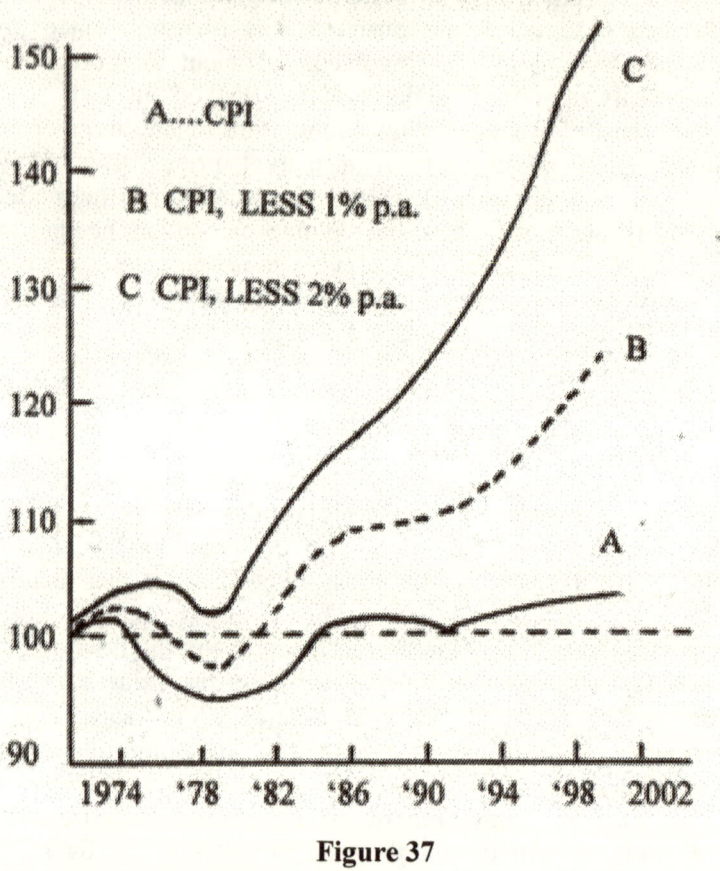

Figure 37

These differences are serious because they affect inflation-indexed entitlements. The Congressional Budget Office reports that each 1% reduction in reported inflation would add $25 billion to the budget surplus each year. Even more serious have been periodic Federal Reserve actions to cool-off an "overheating" economy by raising interest rates and by decreasing the money supply for investments. This syndrome has been repeated again and again over the last several decades resulting in a four year "boom and bust"set of cycles, in which the economy peaks (curiously) just at Presidential election times. Such economic volatility is destructive for sustained investments needed for survival, and each recession takes its toll.

The Bureau of the Census in an analysis of a number of service sector segments, found that productivity increases were 2% to 4% instead of the average 0.4% reported over the previous decade. Also, a Wharton Business School study showed similar 2% to 4% increases when the difference was measured between reported inflation and increases in the return on investment. The Q-factor (Figure 38) is, in effect, a measure of "total" productivity. It is the ratio of the total value of company stocks and bonds in the market, to the replacement costs of the corporate assets involved. Historically, stocks and corporate bonds have sold at about a 70% discount to replacement costs. However, in the second phase of the Kondratieff longwave (1945-1965) the Q-factor rose rapidly responding to heavy investments in new systems and increasing productivity. Then as the third phase of overcapacity began, and profits eroded, the ratio fell back reflecting also the downsizing and restructuring of the 1970's and 1980's.

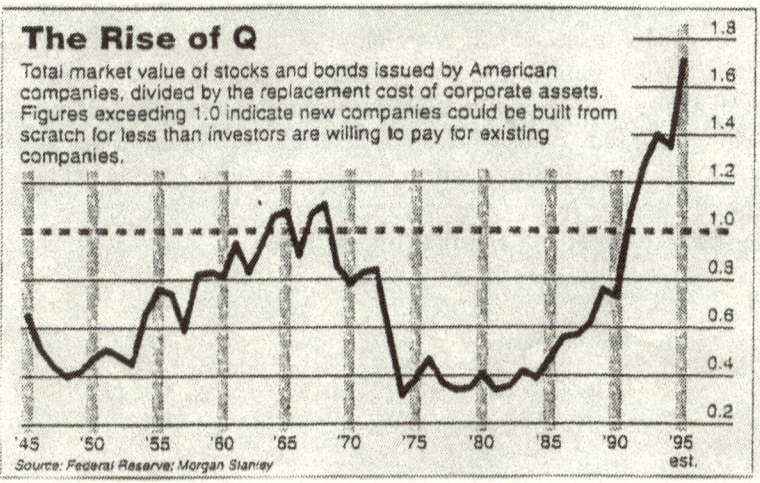

Figure 38

Fortunately, the Economic Recovery Tax Act (ERTA) of 1981 jump-started the entrepreneurial revolution that has more than offset the downsizing. Also, reflecting important increases in technology-driven productivity, the Q-factor now has risen to about 1.9, almost unaffected by the "hysterical" market drop between August and October, 1998. Currently, stocks and corporate bonds are selling for about 75% more than their replacement costs. Consumers, not Government statisticians now establish the relative value of the goods they buy.

Market Valuations and Simulations

The price/earnings (P/E) ratio is a measure of the value-added of an equity, but can fluctuate somewhat erratically with market volatility --- often rising initially in market downturns, as selling lags the reporting of profit erosion, and again when recovery occurs. Also, internet and other rapidly growing businesses, often now are priced one or more years in advance of current earnings, producing very high P.E. ratios. The current value of a business and its P/E is perhaps more accurately supplied by its statistical correlation with its constraint analysis score, which can be used to simulate future rates of growth as well as the current conditions. For example, Intel and Microsoft, with constraint scores of over 100, should be selling in the range of 30-35 times <u>trailing</u> earnings. Expectations of much higher future earnings, and foreign capital now flooding into the U.S. tend to escalate the P/E ratio. (Figure 39)

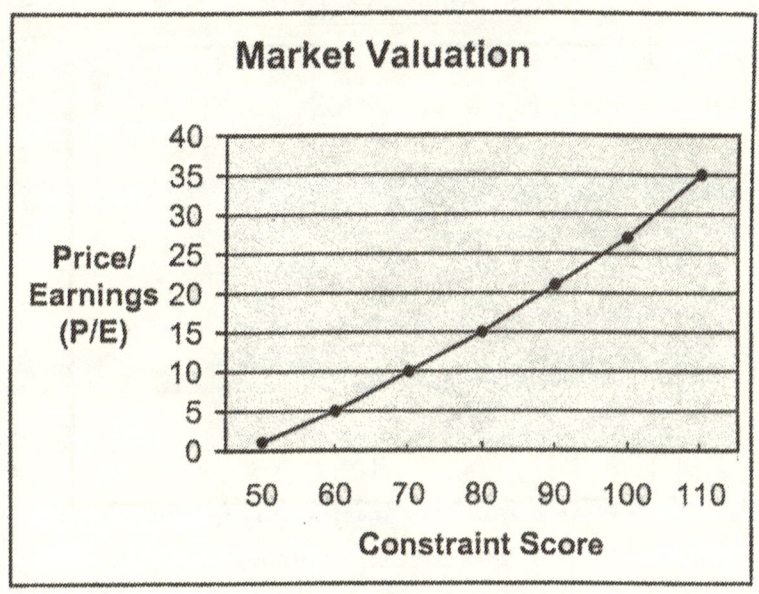

Figure 39

Other Simulations

The average top 500 U.S. company pays about 45% of earnings out in dividends to stockholders, has an ROE of about 15%, and a return on all net assets of about 12% (Figure 40). In this chart, real retained earnings are shown as a function of debt, dividend payout, and inflation, and as they affect the Return on Net Assets Employed (RONAE). With a dividend payout of 45% of RONAE, and 3% (in recent years) inflation, retained earnings are only 3.5% (Figure 41).

Widget Model

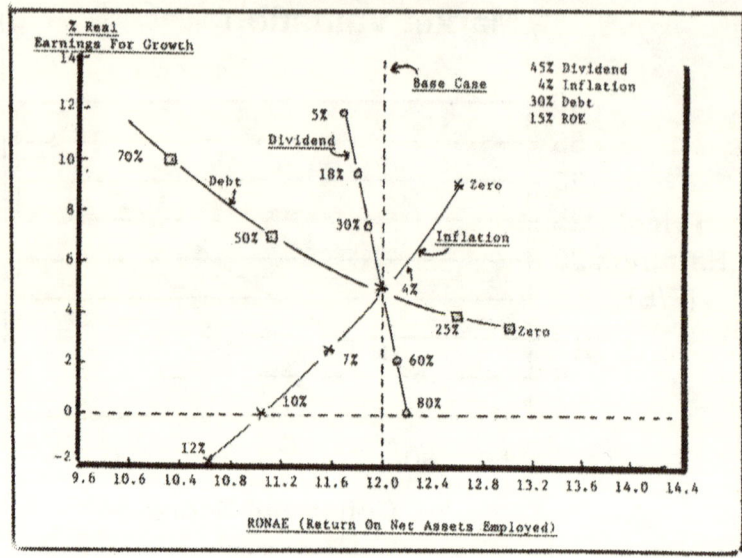

Figure 40

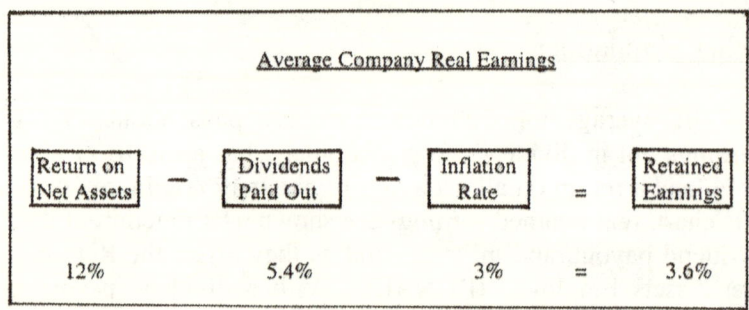

Figure 41

In the 1980's when inflation reached double digits (12%), the average company was actually liquidating its assets at a rate over 5% per year.

Dividend payout, of course, directly depletes the cash flow for additional growth investments. In a sense, it is a tacit admission that a company management cannot find high value-added opportunities for such investments in its current mix of businesses --- and should be considering diversification.

o Westinghouse liquidated its traditional businesses to buy CBS, and no longer exists as a manufacturing company.
o Monsanto has spun off its traditional chemical businesses to become a biotech company focusing on high value-added pharmaceuticals and genetically modified agricultural seeds and herbicides.
o duPont similarly has spun off Connoco, its oil subsidiary, and other low value added businesses to focus on biotech and materials science.

In the past, utilities have been territorially circumscribed with little direct competition, operating as regulated monopolies. With growth limited to demographic changes within their territories, they traditionally have paid high dividends. Deregulation, and permission for private investors to generate electricity and pump it into the grid, now will restructure this industry with uncertain results for dividend payout, let alone survival.

Increased debt increases cash flow for investments, although it decreases RONAE. Strategically, taking on debt can be important for accelerating the development and commercialization, or acquisition, of high value-added opportunities. The risk has been that an economic recession or downturn could reduce cash flow to the point where interest payments could not be met and the company could fail. The stock market tends to downgrade companies whose debt to equity ratios exceed 50%. From a strategic management point of view, quantification of these effects needs to be carefully considered.

Summary

Valuation metrics are critically important for managing any business in the current period of rapid change.

o "If you can't measure it, you probably don't really understand it," and if you don't know your business profile, you may be seriously mismanaging it.

Sensitivity analyses in a graphic format do provide a unique profile of any business operation. Perhaps most importantly, the software involved allows a rapid process of simulation, in which desired end cost/performance results that are desired, can be fed backward to optimize the mix of individual cost, price and volume factors, which would be needed to achieve those ends. This process also then can help focus additional development efforts where they can be most effective.

These metrics highlight the critical importance of knowledge-intensive, high value-added, proprietary operations --- a primary form of increased productivity which is essential for a sustainable competitive advantage. No method of measurement is perfect or without some subjective interpretation, but the Constraint Analysis and the Sensitivity Analysis can provide reality checks.

References

1. Michael Boskin et al "Report to the Senate Finance Committee," <u>New York Times</u> Section H, (12/1/96).

2. Leonard Nakamura, Economist, Federal Reserve Bank of Philadelphia, <u>Business Review</u> (1977); <u>New York Times</u> Section H, (12/1/96).

3. U.S. Department of Commerce, Economic and Statistics Administration, Bureau of Economic Analysis, <u>Quarterly Reports</u>; D. Bruce Merrifield, "Creative Destruction in the New Millenium", <u>J. Technology Management</u> Vol 4, pp 1-9 (1997).

4. Bureau of Census Report (CPI-UXI), 1994.

5. Francis X. Frei, Patrick J. Naoker, Larry W. Hunter, "Performance in Consumer Financial Services" <u>Working Paper</u>, Wharton School of Business pp 95-103.

KEY CONCEPTS TO REVIEW

- Develop the sensitivity profile of a business or profit center with which you are familiar; what innovative ideas could further enhance the ROI-DCF, focusing on the most sensitive factors in the profile?
- If the ROI-DCF is less than 20% and after tax profits are less than 10%, what mix of changes would be required to achieve these values. Would a technical breakthrough be required? What would be the possibility of such an advance in the technology?
- What P/E value would this business have, and what is the likelihood that this business has or can have a sustainable competitive advantage?
- Why is the "economic surplus" factor in measuring productivity (and therefore also inflation) so important relative to other factors involved in productivity?
- Why is inflation a direct tax on equity?

CHAPTER V

INNOVATION DRIVEN CONTINUOUS CORPORATE RENEWAL

Perspective

Over the next decade or two, the need will accelerate in every country and in every organization for both entrepreneurial new-business formation, and for continuous corporate renewal. These two processes involve different specialized disciplines, often not well understood. They apply to both already industrialized nations, and to the lesser developed countries (LDC's) where about 85% of world populations live. Hernando deSoto, a Peruvian, has written a book, based on a seven year study of Latin American countries. His conclusion is that the primary definition of an LDC is "one where entrepreneurial activity is illegal." Fortunately, excellent models for initiating new small business creation processes in LDC's has been demonstrated, and now need to be widely replicated (see Chapter VII).

Industrialized nations also need to accelerate the corporate renewal process and the generation of entrepreneural new small businesses. Sadly, many old-line companies in the U.S., Europe and elsewhere have failed to encourage an intrapreneurial process, even though latent creativity almost always exists in every organization. As a result, if change eventually comes, it usually comes from outside the organization --- under duress. This is Joseph Schumpeter's "process of creative destruction," but is one where the primary benefits usually accrue to an outside innovator, not to the acquiring organization, which only belatedly attempts to downsize, restructure and become a fast-follower.

Early in the 20th century, the pace of discovery was much slower, and product and process life cycles often involved a decade or more. The fast-follower strategy then was viable. A company with superior marketing and distribution, and deep pockets, could mount a crash program to develop a competitive product, and then overwhelm the smaller innovator.

- o IBM did not "recognize" the potential for personal computers, until Apple had such remarkable success. A crash program at IBM developed a different architecture and a complex but inferior software (Os/2). But IBM then opened up its architecture to stimulate software development by others, and for a time appeared to be very successful. However, the open architecture also stimulated dozens of PC clones which now have become dominant, and IBM, which might have been the dominant first-mover, now has only about 10% of the PC market.

Increasingly, a first-mover with a strongly proprietary product or process will be the most successful. But even the first-mover will need to mount an ongoing vigorous process of further innovation, to sustain a competitive advantage. Intel has maintained about an 80% market share in processors, but only by developing a new generation chip every two or three years. This is a particularly stark example of life cycle compression --- a major new factor in corporate management.

Life Cycle Patterns

A typical life cycle pattern for an important product or process has traditionally had a pattern as shown in Figure 42.

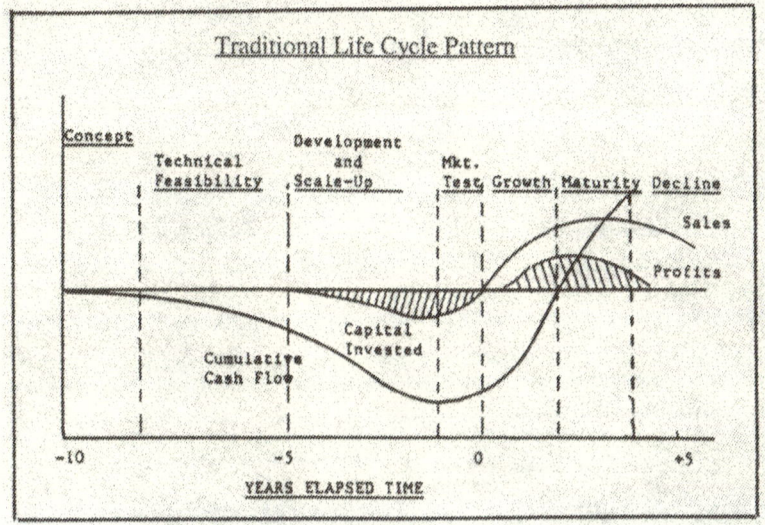

Figure 42

In the initial stages, a long period of negative cash flow results during development, scale-up, and initial production. Positive cash flows finally are reached about the time the product or process reaches maturity. Sales are still growing, but profits have peaked. This is the time when a next-generation system also should have been ready for introduction, sustained by the cash being thrown off by the first-generation product.

This pattern, obviously, is no longer viable, because life cycles now have collapsed to just a few years in many industries. In the past, the life cycle has been characterized by an S-curve which has four stages. The first stage (Figure 43), involves the initial introduction of an innovation, such as the Apple Computer. This act then stimulates the fast followers who swarm into the market with different versions of the original (IBM, Dell, Compaq). A period of dynamic process development ensues. In the third period, however, a dominant design develops, which because of economies of scale tends to preclude further radical developments, even though they may be superior. Instead, competition degenerates into adding more "bells and whistles."

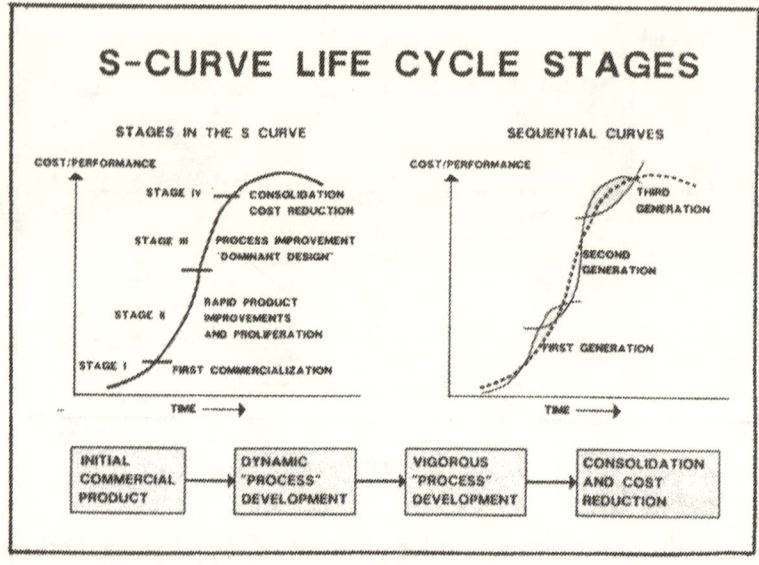

Figure 43

o The Betamax video recorder was technically superior to the VHS, but because of an aggressive marketing-licensing strategy, the VHS established the dominant design, and won the battle.

Finally, in the fourth stage, the market consolidates to a few large competitors, who now focus on cost reductions. As margins erode, excess capacity usually results, and the next-generation system may be emerging. However, unfortunately, this next-generation system usually has not been developed by existing competitors, but by a new competitor using much different technology often requiring a new "core competency." Moreover, S-curve patterns now have collapsed from decades to just a few years, with the result that the third and fourth stages may never be reached, before new innovations obsolete the old.

This collapsing pattern is illustrated in Figure 44 for switching systems. Cycle time reduction then becomes an overriding need as illustrated in Figure 45.

Sadly, in many companies, an entrenched bureaucracy (the so-called "core competency") has had time to develop during the first 3 stages. This core competency vigorously resists change, while discounting any threat. Instead, it mounts a frenetic effort to further improve the older existing technology to no avail.

- o The greatest advances in sailing ship technology occured after Robert Fulton invented the steamboat. And perhaps even one day, fibre optic cables and satellites will finally obsolete the twisted pair of copper wires, in spite of "valiant" current efforts to increase their band-width. Of course, rear guard actions such as these often are necessary to buy time to recover from the original lack of vision and the sub-sequent resistance to change. However, much to be preferred is an always ongoing and vigorous process of anticipating change accompanied by a carefully focused process of <u>intra</u>preneurial renewal, focused on future needs

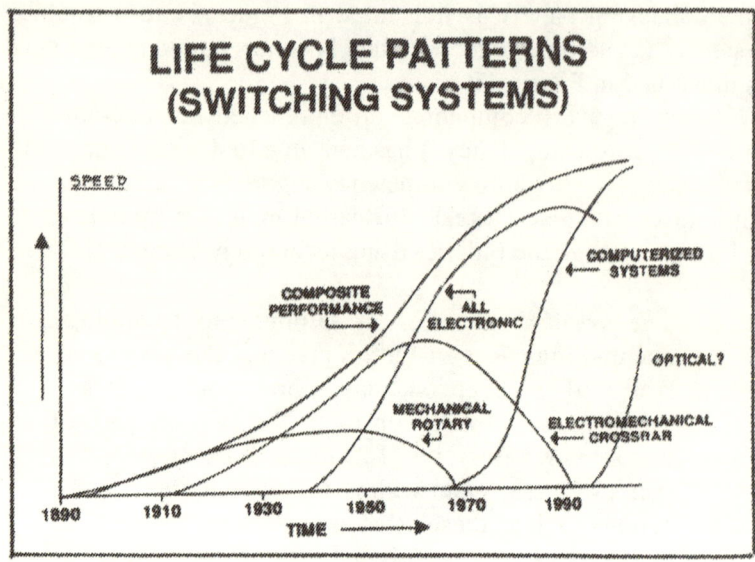

Figure 44

Forecasting The Future
―――――――――――

Misdirected efforts waste both time and money, and also can discredit internal development efforts as an important element in continuous renewal. Therefore, it is important that such efforts be not only validated in advance by screening methodologies such as the "Constraint Analysis," but also be focused, if possible, on an understanding of future trends. The S-curve patterns of change illustrated in Figure 43, often can point to such trends, restructuring most industries.

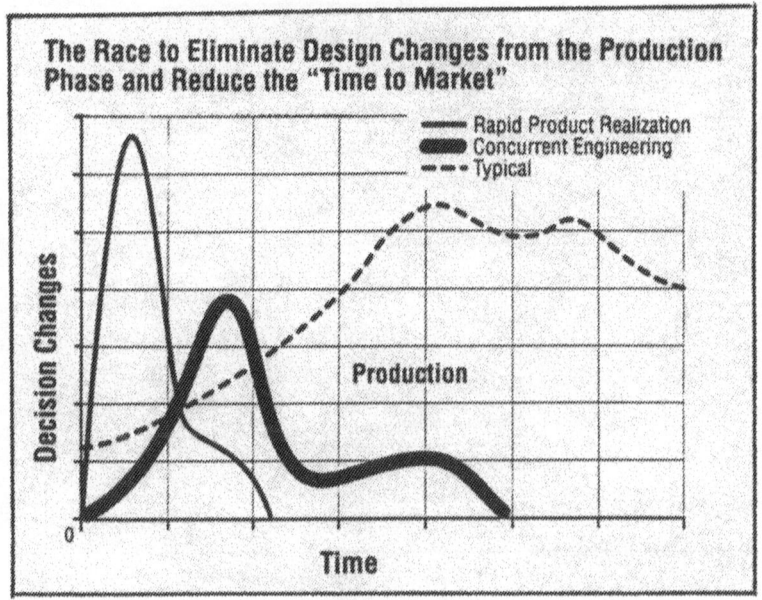

Figure 45

o <u>The Future of Education</u>

In the 1700's, about 90% of all U.S. citizens lived on farms, with their educational needs served by the "little red schoolhouse" in a fragmented agricultural community. One teacher often taught all subjects in all grades. Instruction was interrupted in the summers, so that the children could work on the farms. (This pattern still persists, although only 2% of the U.S. population now are farmers.)

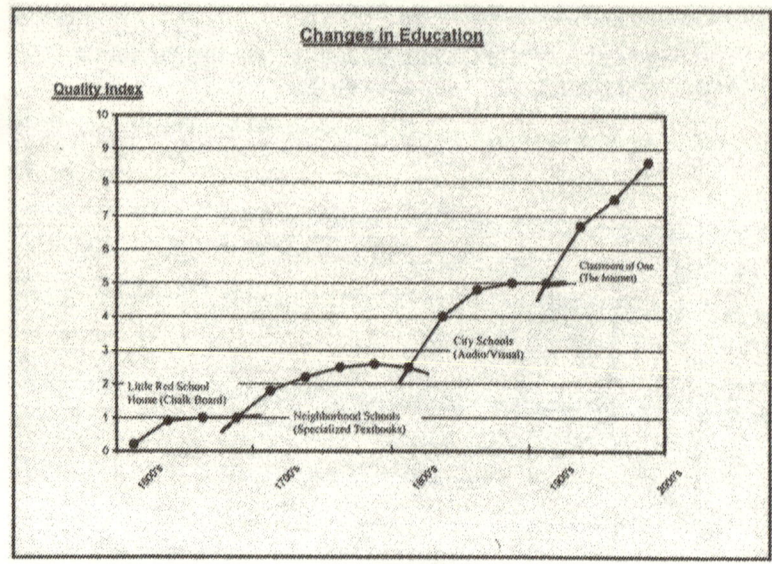

Figure 46

Although the little red schoolhouse may have satisfied many of the needs of an agrarian economy, a steady process of urbanization in the last half of the 1800's erected new demands for skills and knowledge. Neighborhood schools emerged in towns and villages, which could provide more specialized teaching over a wider spectrum of subjects (history, civics, science, geography, manual arts, in addition to reading, writing, and arithmetic). In the 1900's, large cities developed, giving rise to centralized school districts, where the driving force now became less focused on the quality of education than on possible economies of scale via standardized curricula, books, and audio-visual aids Figure 46.

Unfortunately, this process became increasingly Government subsidized and therefore, bureaucratically controlled. Currently, on average, about two-thirds of all appropriated public school funding is siphoned-off by the bureaucracy. For example, the District of Columbia reports the highest expenditures per capita in the U.S. but rates among the very lowest on standardized tests.

This is at a time when the primary driving forces are for an even higher quality of education, and for life-long continuous reskilling. Increased quality of education will be provided, but not likely by the current system.

Instead, the need will be met increasingly by the current revolution in communications, which already is beginning to by-pass the entrenched bureaucracy. The "schoolroom of one" now is remerging via computers, fibre optic cables, wireless systems and the Internet. This technology has made available almost unlimited access to diverse data bases, including the Library of Congress. One driving force will involve the need for life-long continuous skilling and reskilling, since any set of skills now can become obsolescent in 5 to 10 years. This is a new frontier for the educational process which once was considered "complete" following the formal education period.

Another driving force of even greater magniturde will involve the demand for education by billions of people in developing countries. The first U.S. Economic Mission to China in 1979, (following signing of a U.S. Peoples Republic Treaty) initiated the Chinese television school, from which tens of thousands of Chinese now graduate each year --- a beginning model for other countries. Interactive video education in real time via the Inernet soon will begin to bring education to all "corners" of the earth for the first time in history. And provide entrepreneurial opportunities not before possible.

o   The Future of Communications

For most of the 10,000 years of civilization the process of communications was limited to the speed of a horse, a sailing ship and the carrier pigeon. American Indians used smoke signals, and semaphore flags were used between ships at sea, but it wasn't until the pony express was started that "scheduled distance" communication (though very limited) was possible. The telegraph developed by Samuel Morse in 1837, and the telephone by Alexander Graham Bell in 1876, began the modern era of affordable long distance communication --- still limited, however, by the speed and volume of electrons transmitted by a twisted pair of copper wires. Nevertheless, transatlantic cables and national networks of telephone lines brought the industrial nation together in real time (Figure 47).

A further revolution now is in progress driven by the forces of cost, speed, and by bandwidth (the volume of data transmitted per unit of time). As bandwidth continues to increase exponentially and costs fall almost as rapidly, the copper wire and billions of dollars in supporting investments will become obsolete. Fibre optic cables and satellite (wireless) communications already transmit digitized and compressed information at the speed of light anywhere in the world. The Internet already makes available unlimited sources of data and information in any living room. Encrypted personal files, documents and financial records may soon be stored by individuals on the Internet for selective access, using small mobile inexpensive "dumb" terminals from any location. High clarity video telephony may become available at negligible cost on any desktop, TV set, or

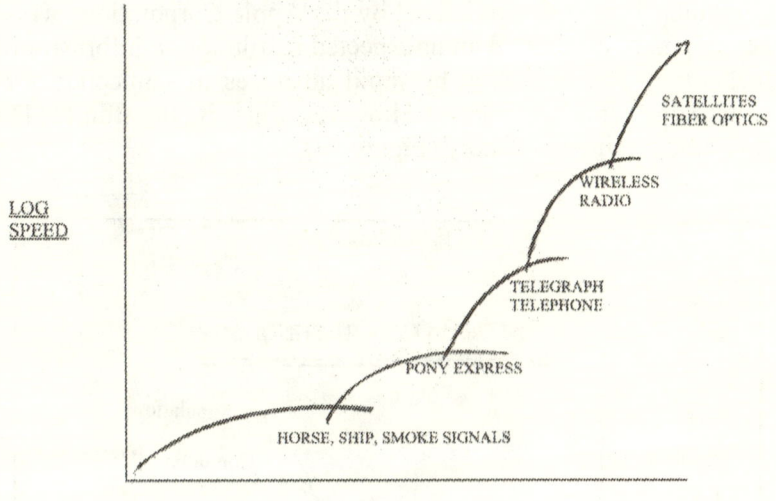

Figure 47

bedside table, with high fidelity contact anywhere in the world. Immediate access likely also will develop for on-line expert legal, financial, educational and medical diagnostics (the office of one). On-line shopping for next-day delivery from the manufacturer, will increasingly by-pass distributors and many retail outlets, but will be a bonanza for delivery businesses. Rapid color printing already available, may by-pass or alter other forms of communication (newspaper, magazines, TV broadcasts) as the Internet provides selective up-to-date customized reports on demand, through selected services --- an excellent example of Schumpeter's principle of "creative destruction."

o Information Technology (IT)

The Palo Alto Research Laboratories of the Xerox Company first developed an early prototype of the modern personal computer, later commercialized by the Apple Corporation. This development ushered in an unexpected revolution in information technology further driven by rapid advances in semiconductor technology and software. However, this is the fourth IT revolution in human history (Figure 48).

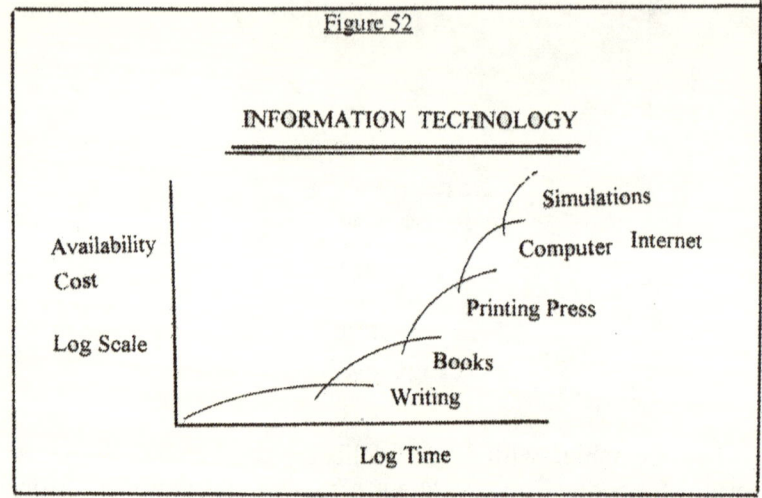

Figure 48

The first one involved the invention of writing in Mesopotamia around 3000 to 4000 B.C. (later independently reinvented in China about 2000 B.C.). The second IT revolution followed the invention of written books, also about 1300 B.C. in China and later again independently, in Greece about 500 B.C. (to chronicle Homer's epics, only recited until then.) By the 1400s some 10,000 monks in thousands of monasteries labored six days a week copying books by hand in Latin

However, by the year 1500 A.D. these monks were unemployed as a result of a third revolution brought about by Gutenberg's invention of the printing press in 1450 A.D., and by the contemporaneous invention of engraving, which made possible illustrated books. Five hundred years later the current IT revolution has further reduced the cost and increased the availability of information by orders of magnitude, aided by fibre optic cables and satellite transmission. So far, this revolution has been dominated by advances in semiconductor technology, integrated circuits and software, primarily focused on increasing the productivity of internal operations.

A fifth revolution now may be beginning in which this relatively narrow focus will expand to the integration of data and information into a much higher value-added strategic focus on creation of new wealth and expanded opportunities. More specifically, data have little value alone until they are integrated into useful (knowledge-intensive) patterns, which then can lead to strategically useful decisions and actions, or to new avenues of experimentation, not seen before. The most important discoveries often are made at the interface between several different disciplines. For example, some of the recent advances in medical engineering have been based on advances in material sciences, combined with micro-analytical and imaging techniques.

o <u>Medicine and Biogenetics</u>

For most of human history, life spans have been cut short by disease, poor nutrition, and accidents, that now are routinely cured or treatable. Herbal medicines were beneficial and recently have been found to have a sientific basis. For example, the American Indians warded off tooth decay by chewing on an indigenous bark. This bark now has been found to contain a member of the penicillin family, and has been incorporated into a commercial toothpaste.

However, a first stage of "modern medicine" did not occur until Pasteur and others demonstrated the connection between bacteria and disease. Pasteur then produced the first cure for rabies. A more sophisticated stage of medical investigation began with Fleming's discovery of penicillin in 1928, and its commercialization during World War II. The sulfa drugs and other antibiotics followed, saving countless wounded.

Subsequent development of vaccines, heart disease drugs, and even newer antibiotics now have virtually eliminated many of the scourges of history and prolonged the life span. However, concurrent with these advances has been spectacular progress in medical engineering. Surgeons, engineers and material scientists have collaborated to provide replacement parts for hips, knees, hearts, livers and other organs. Cataract surgery, angioplasty, heart pacemakers, and defibrillators have both extended and increased the quality of life of senior citizens.

An even more remarkable era now is beginning. It involves "cellular biogenetics" and "tissue engineering." Lab-grown bones, cartilage, skin, blood vessels, livers, pancreases, breasts, ears, fingers, nerves, and tooth enamel now are in advanced testing and beginning use. The potential is one of keeping people young and healthy for a very long time. Immune rejection currently is being solved by encapsulating donor cells in porous membranes, and a universal "stem" or donor cell for all tissues may be a possibility. DNA mapping can reveal genetic deficiencies for early correction, and provide a DNA donor pool for couples desiring "designer babies," or even cloned individuals, raising serious ethical considerations never before addressed.

From an industrial point of view, the insatiable demand for a longer healthy and more "productive" life will continue to drive developments in this area.

Very large increases in productivity already are resulting from the "combinatorial screening" of thousands of new chemical entities, and major advances will continue in medical and tissue engineering. More specifically, genetic manipulation of plants and animals followed by cloning of superior species, will become a rapidly growing business. Gene pools for "designer species," including humans are inevitable. Already, the first human species has been cloned, raising serious ethical considerations.

o   <u>Banking and Financial Services</u>

Recently, a few smart traders on Wall Street, using sophisticated computer-assisted mathematics, and instantaneous communications systems, have undercut central bank controls of capital flows, interest and exchange rates to precipitate the Asian meltdown. They have taken advantage of, and have made enormous profits at the expense of already vulnerable multinational companies, and poorly managed and economically unstable governments. Companies with a high percentage of sales in foreign countries have been especially vulnerable, as traders whipsaw them by manipulating exchange rates.

- o Andrew Krieger at the Bankers Trust Co. used options to sell short the entire money supply of New Zealand, making over $300 million in one year for Bankers Trust.
- o Speculators attacking the Thailand Baht and currencies in Indonesia and other Asian countries caused an international panic --- taking advantage of lags in accounting for foreign currency exchanges. Daily turnover is about $1.3 trillion, compared with about half that amount currently held in reserves by all the richest countries combined.

The loss of financial sovereignty involved, likely will extend to other nations as well, emphaszing the order of magnitude advantage of knowledge-intensive advanced technical systems --- a long way from the "green eyeshade" era of not too long ago. Loss of economic sovereignty also will result, as trade barriers slowly fall, and are by-passed by strategic alliances, driven by the need for rapid market penetration for products that have a limited life cycle. Novel forms of organization and management will be required to implement this process (see Chapter VII).

Steps Involved in Continuous Renewal

Continuous renewal will be required for survival in a hyper-competitive global marketplace, but also will be enabled by historically an unprecedented explosion of advanced technology. However, the process must start with a "current-situation" or "bench-marking" analysis, in which all current operations are measured against global competition, both for near-term and longer-term viability. The Constraint Analysis and the Sensitivity Analysis provide useful tools for doing this. Subsequent steps (Figure 49) continue with a projection of desired financials (sales and profit growth, return on equity and after-tax profit targets, degree of diversification etc.) over the next five and ten year periods. Only then can alternative radical improvement and new business options be considered that might achieve such goals, and provide a sustainable competitive advantage. Finally, a strategic plan can be constructed incorporating a mix of initiatives, followed by detailed business plans that define the skills and resources needed and the time-based access to those capabilities for each profit center, and product process or service.

Steps In Continuous Renewal

- Current-Situation Analysis
- Five and Ten Year Visions
- Option Analysis of Pathways
- The Strategic Plan
- Detailed Business Plans
- Allocation of Resources

Figure 49

It is important to appreciate that incremental improvements of existing operations, alone, cannot suffice. Instead, a much more radical course of action will be required. These courses of action should always <u>first</u> be focused on the possibilities of continued use or rejuvenation of existing core competencies in production, marketing and distribution which can telescope the time for rapid market penetration of new systems. Several models are apparent:

(1) <u>Radical Transformation of a Key Component</u>

Rejuvenation of an obsolescing product or process (and its core competency) sometimes can be achieved by a radical (5 to 10 times factor) improvement in one limiting component. For example, currently available batteries store useful amounts of electricity, but are notoriously deficient in their ability to deliver large amounts of power in a short time, without damaging the battery and shortening its life. As a result, they often must be over-designed at considerable cost, to somewhat minimize this disadvantage. The National Institue of Standards and Technology (NIST) has identified surge or preminum power as a critical component that would not only accelerate the viability of electric vehicle operation (notoriously underpowered), but also significantly increase the performance of many other electrically powered products (power tools, cellular phones, defibrillators, airbags, etc.).

Another example, is the development of advanced electrical motors by the Reliance Division of Rockwell, and the development by Pirelli North America of electrical distribution cables using high temperature superconducting (HTS) wires --- major advances which could restructure those industries. However, the radical component-improvement strategy is not always possible, and might not be sufficient. Therefore other strategies also need to be considered.

(2) <u>Radical Transformation of an Entire Existing System</u>

An excellent example of this strategy is provided by Intel, which has developed a next-generation processor every two or three years, while still utilizing the same (evolving) core competency in technical manufacturing and marketing capabilities. Also, pharmaceutical companies have continually developed new composition of matter drugs which build on existing core competencies, while developing new techniques such as those involved in combinatorial synthesis and screening. The payoffs can be enormous, but the effort must be unrelenting.

(3) <u>Radical Transformation Requiring New Skills and Resources</u>

One example of this strategy involves the 3M Company which has continually developed an enormous array of diversified products and processes, often requiring new core competencies. Also, General Electric, ("the appliance company") now receives about 40% of its profits from financial services. This important G.E. business started in a very small way through the need to finance time purchases of large appliances, and now is a full-service business with its own totally unique core competency.

A different example involved Westinghouse, which bought CBS, and then spun off all the Westinghouse operations --- (with the demise of another famous corporate name). In a different example, Monsanto, building from its herbicide business into genetically modified crops, now has spun off its conventional chemical business ("Solutia"), to focus on both agriculture and pharmaceuticals in a biochemical core competency. Dupont and other chemical companies are also following this path.

However, not all companies can make such radical transformations by themselves, and often an interesting in-house discovery, that does not fit existing capabilites, therefore is shelved. In fact, the "shelves" of most companies are cluttered with partially developed product and processes --- which could have been profitable operations in a joint venture or licensing arrangement with another company, that had the missing capabilities.

o   The Rogers Company was developing an important advance in flexible interconnect systems, but the cash drain and lack of in-place marketing impelled the company to form a joint venture with AMP to commercialize the technology. Rogers provides proprietary materials to the joint venture.

Both licensing in and out, as well as joint venture formation should be considered in the situation-analysis, strategic-planning process for every existing operation. Central to this form of option-analysis, is the need for a very effective and ongoing intelligence function, that searches world technical, patent, and commercial literature for innovative discoveries and developments. Of particular value often are those at the interface of in-house disciplines with non-captive disciplines. Searchers must be highly competent technically and imaginative enough to recognize possible fits with, and extensions of, current operations --- data for the strategic plan.

The Strategic Plan

Following earlier steps involving the benchmarking, financial projection, and world search process, a strategic plan then can be assembled. It involves several additional steps (Figure 50). The first step involves reducing the data base for each possible initiative to a prototype business operation in the form of a market segment analysis. This analysis (Figure 51) identifies the leading competitors and the best technology currently available for each market application in the business areas under consideration. It also identifies current weaknesses and deficiencies of that technology as it attempts to serve the customer needs involved. Finally, it attempts to identify at least theoretical options for radical imporvement, the feasibility of doing so, and the resourses that might be needed.

Elements of the Strategic Plan

- Generation of Alternative Options
- Detailed Market Segmentation
- Priority Analysis
- Decision Tree Analysis
- Final Plan

Figure 50

Market Segments	Current Volume Sales	Units	5 Year Growth	Competitors How Active	Technology Now Used	Deficiencies Existing	Opportunities For Innov.
1.							
2.							
3.							
4.							
5.							

Market Segment Analysis

Figure 51

Constraint Analysis scores need to be developed both for the business as it is, and as it would be if a major advance could be achieved, and the probability of doing so estimated. From this sort of analysis, priorities can be assigned, understanding that an existing deficiency for which there is no immediate solution might appear at any time. The resulting profile can be charted as in figure 52. In this chart, profit centers A through F had Constraint Analysis scores as shown. There were no growth businesses, and several (D, E, and F) were candidates for divestiture.

This was quite a shock to the top management, and the initial response was one of denial. However, a special task force confirmed the results, and the resulting "agonizing reappraisal" began. Rejuvenation of one core competency was achieved through a "radical component" strategy, another through in-licensing of an advanced development that could use the existing core competency. However, in the decision tree evaluation, two of the three divestiture candidates were spun off, and the third down-sized and then merged into a joint venture with another company that had an advanced component. The sixth profit center was maintained as a cash cow to fund development of the first two.

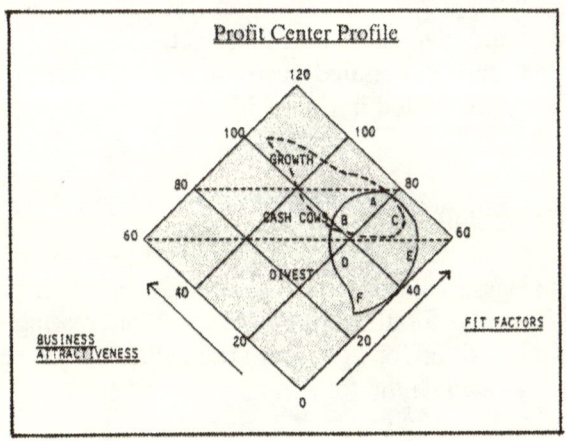

Figure 52

EXHIBIT III

DECISION TREE EVALUATION

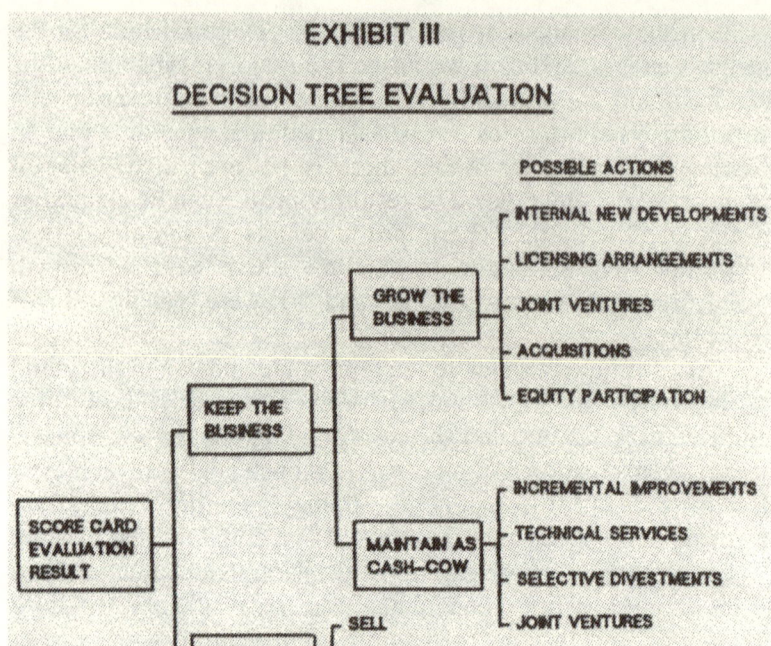

Figure 53

The strategic plan settled on these actions, which then were implemented through detailed business plans. A useful decision tree analysis is illustrated in figure 53

The Business Plan

The business plan translates the strategic plan into a detailed time-based process for allocating resources, for creating strategic allinces if desired, or for licensing arrangements. The elements of this process include the following:

o   The Product, Process or Service

The nature of the business involved is described in terms of its currently perceived competitive advantage and the sustainability of that advantage. Also projected are growth potential, risk distribution, political and social factors that might add or detract from its viability, and the availabity of resources needed.

o   The Market

Segments of the market are described in terms of sales volume, potential profitability, the ease and order of entry and the degree of risk distribution involved.

o   The Technology

The nature of the interfacing technologies involved are described in terms of the skills required, the degree of proprietary character (leading to a competitive advantage), and the opportunities for continued development to sustain the competitive advantage.

o   Production Requirements

Pilot plant, interim production, and full scale production requirements, capital availability, and skills and resources needed, are described. Unit cost projections should be projected at each level of scale-up, and the degree of flexibility defined for a given platform to meet diverse specifications.

o   Intellectual Property

Patents and copyrights, issued and applied for, are detailed in terms of (1) fundamental disclosures, broadly filed in many countries, (2) strongly supportive disclosures, filed in only the primary industrialized countreis, (3) "picket" disclosures registered only in the

U.S. to prevent competitors from blocking access to niche areas, and (4) non-disclosed proprietary information, held confidential.

o   Risks and Issues

Possible risks and issues need to be described that could have a material effect on the business, together with the likelihood of their occurance and remedial initiatives if they should occur.

o   Financial Projections

Detailed 5 year financials are tabulated showing sales and profit growth unit and SG&A costs, capital requirements and scheduling, as well as cash flow and net present value projections, discounted 25% to 40%.

Summary

Continuous corporate renewal now is a requirement for survival, let alone sustainable profitable growth. Incremental improvement of existing operations each year, though important, will not suffice. Instead, significantly radical transformations will be necessary (a 5 to 10 times cost/performance degree of improvement). Options include radical improvements of a key component or of an entire system which can continue to utlize existing core competencies (technical, production, marketing, distribution); or alternatively may require development of entirely new businesses that need different core competencies. A combination of all of these may be necessary. Downsizing, restructuring and divestiture, as well as licensing and formation of strategic alliances are important options. The procedures and disciplines required are detailed in a multiple step process.

References

1. H. DeSoto, "El Otro Sendero: la Revolucion Informal" Peru, 1986: Also, 1980-86 study by the Instituto Liberato y Democracia (ILD).

2. D. Bruce Merrifield, "A Modern Marshall Plan," <u>J. Business Venturing</u> p. 231- 236 (1991).

3. R. N. Foster "Innovation and the Attacker's Advantage" NY Summit Books
i. (1936).

4. R. N. Becker, L. M. Speltz "Putting the S-Curve to Work," <u>Research Management</u> Sept/Oct. (1983).

5. M. M. Buechner, "Virtual Clasroom" <u>Time Digital</u>, Sept. 7 1998.

6. D. Bruce Merrifield, "Creative Destruction I the New Millenium," <u>J. Tech Management</u> 4, No.1, pp 1-9 (1997).

7. D. Burch, A. Hellerman, "Time Table of Technology," Simon & Schuster (1995)

8. A. Milman, "The Vandal's Crown": How Rebel Currency Traders Overthrew the World's Central Banks" <u>The Free Press</u> (1995).

KEY CONCEPTS TO REVIEW

1. What are the advantages and disadvantages of a strong core competency, and why have they been instrumental in the demise of so many famous corporate names?

2. Why will incremental improvements each year no longer assure corporate survival? What alternative strategies need to be implemented?

3. Life cycle compression to a year or two in many consumer electronics and software businesses now is not uncommon. What does it take to develop and maintain a competitive advantage in such areas. Are these business area you want to be involved in?

4. Analyze a small business or profit center of a company with which you are familiar. Develop a Constraint Analysis score, and a Sensitivity Analysis for the business, and then project a 5 year hypothetical strategic plan to achieve a 20% ROE and 10% after tax profits for the business. Consider radical component or system innovations that theoretically might be necessary.

5. Forecast the future of this business in ten years.

CHAPTER VI

MANAGEMENT OF THE TECHNICAL FUNCTION

Perspective

The entrepreneur or intrapreneur, is societies agent of both change and growth who creates new wealth and renews a nation's industrial base. Moreover, in the current hyper-competitive global economy, the expert management of the innovation process has become increasingly important for survival. Unfortunately both an environment conducive to risk taking, and the specialized management skills needed, often have been lacking.

Particularly noteworthy have been the Marxist-socialist centralized command-control economies, which have virtually outlawed entrepreneurship and individual initiative, with predictable results. Also, many bureaucratically encumbered U.S. and other companies have failed, because they too have stifled the intrapreneurial function, and fallen behind global competition. High taxes and burdensome regulatory policies have been detriments to entrepreneurial investments, but perhaps most importantly, the specialized management skills have been missing.

Fortunately, U.S. companies can build on an extraordinary "goldmine" of advanced technology (the "critical technologies"), which have uniquely developed in U.S. laboratories over the last decade or two. Basic research discoveries are the "seed corn" for downstream commercial operations. Recent bibliometric studies now have documented the direct correlation between the two. However, a basic research discovery is a very long way from the marketplace, and its further development, scale-up and commercialization requires expert management.

The Innovation Process

Innovation is not a one-time event, but rather is an exceedingly complex, interactive, distributed and non-linear sequence, in which new ideas can arise at any point in a progressive chain of discovery, development, pilot demonstration, production and marketing, and then feed back to earlier stages, often resulting in a redirection of the original thrust of the program (Figure 54). Consequently, innovation management requires considerable flexibility.

Innovation Pipeline

Concurrent Functions ↓	Idea Generated	Technical Feasibility	Development Stages	Pilot Scale	Interim Production	Commercial Operation
Technical	→					
Marketing	→	Go / No Go		Go / No Go	Go / No Go	Go / No Go	Go / No Go
Legal	→					
Financial	→					
Production	→					

[← Fundamental Research (10% of Total Cost) →] [← Further Development and Scale-Up (90% of the Cost) →] [Automation (More $)^X]

Figure 54

Also, after an initial discovery has been made, about 90% of the costs of further development, scaleup, and interim production, are still ahead. These risk investments then often are followed by about ten times that amount required for volume production and commercialization.

Moreover, the skills and resources needed to develop and commercialize a next-generation system frequently do not reside in a single organization, or report to a single person. Importantly, they also may be widely dispersed geographically. However, the management of such dispersed capabilities still requires real-time coordination, now increasingly feasible through electronic communications. Also, formation of strategic alliances often will be required to reach global markets (see Chapter VII), adding another dimension to this sophisticated management process. Finally, risk funding always is a problem, particularly because a gap in funding exists for the earliest stages of development (Figure 55). The Small Business Innovation Research (SBIR) grants and the Advanced Technology program (ATP) grants have been created to partially fill this gap. But both of these combined fund perhaps one out of one hundred viable opportunities. Even then, the available funding is frequently insufficient to demonstrate proof of commercial viability. Consequently, many important discoveries have taken many years to commercialize:

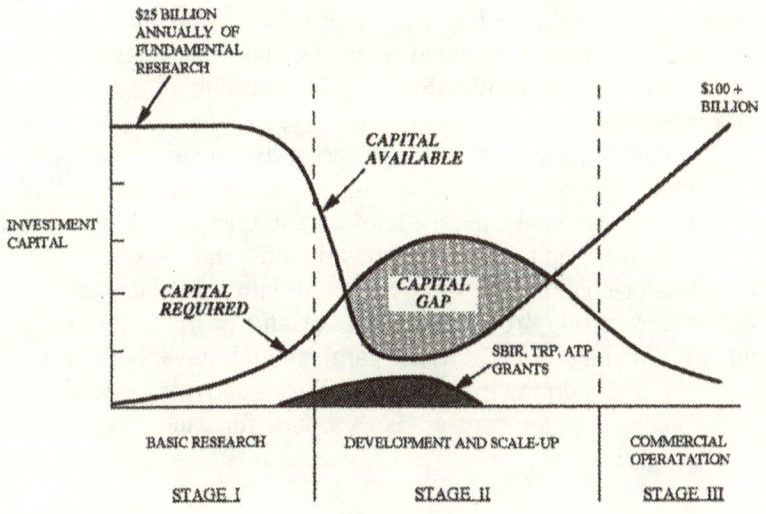

Figure 55

- An IBM Zurich laboratory discovered High Temperature Superconductivity (HTS) in 1986, but more than a decade later, no significant commercial applications have resulted, because very few, if any, companies, alone, can hold captive all the skills and resources needed or, alone, can justify the long negative cash flows involved in their further development. Recently the Department of Energy has catalyzed the formation of several vertically-integrated industry-led, industry-managed consortia around industry-selected applications, and has seed-funded the first two of three stages of development, to reduce the risks. When successful, the applications involved (power line cables, large scale electrical energy storage, motors, fault current limiters), likely will restructure their industries, some with profound effects.

The management process itself involves a critical path (see attached Figure 56) the first step of which is to determine that the technology has not already been patented or copyrighted by someone else. Assuming that a proprietary position can be achieved, the market segment analyses and constraint analyses can lead to prioritization and subsequent milestone determinations, and a strategic plan, as shown. Often this process will require formation of vertically integrated consortia or alliances such as the HTS examples. Consortia must include not only the technical capabilities, but also component-suppliers, an integrator, and globally positioned end users. The "coordinator-champion" who helps initiate and integrate the programs resulting from the corporate and profit center plans, and who manages the critical path, should have both strong technical and administrative capabilities, and also should be supported by a competent advisory board for each program, or set of programs.

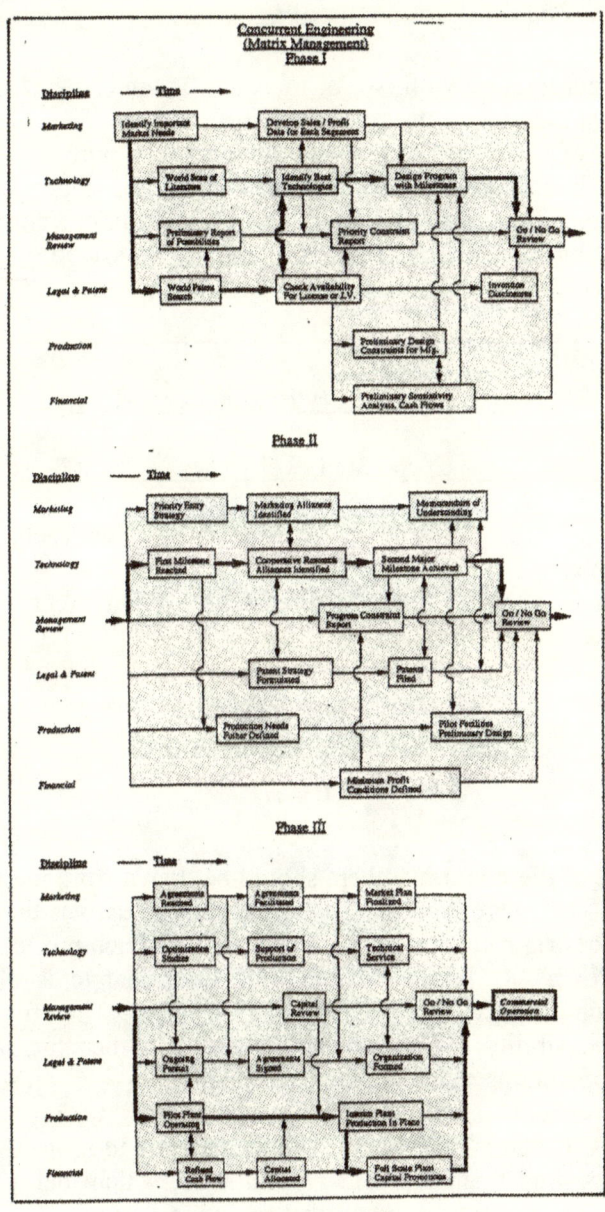

Figure 56

Advisory Boards

In a corporation with two or more profit centers, each profit center should form its own advisory board. The General Manager of the profit center should be the Chairman of the advisory board which also should include the managers of marketing, production, and technology. In addition, corporate legal (patent) and financial representation is advisable, together with the corporate Vice President of Technology (Figure 57).

Profit Center Advisory Board Composition		
Function	Corporate Level	Profit Center
Technology	Corp. Vice President	Mgr. Tech.
Legal (Patents)	Patent Counsel	-
Financial	Corp. Vice President	Dir. Acct.
Marketing	-	Dir. Mkt.
Production	-	Mgr. Prod.
Board Chairman	-	Gen. Mgr.

Figure 57

Most of the board members should be drawn from the profit centers --- to assure vigorous support for any initiatives that they approve or originate, and then are undertaken. Each profit center has to "own" its future. Along this line, change is always resisted unless there is a clear need to change. Therefore, the first responsibility of the advisory board is to benchmark it's current operations against global competition --- to erase any illusions about sustainable competitiveness without new initiatives, if that is necessary. The next step is to project 5 and 10 year desired financials and growth rates, which then can be backed into a strategic plan that could achieve the desired results.

A degree of corporate seed funding (for example, 75% to proof of concept, 50% to prove commercial viability), is warranted for profit center programs that might meet corporate guidelines for profitability and return on equity. However, the profit center P&L should cover all costs once commercial viability has been demonstrated, including costs of further incremental improvements, marketing, sales services and interim production. Subsequent major investments for volume production always are corporate responsibilities, requiring corporate board approval.

Flexible Computer-Integrated Manufacturing

Henry Ford ushered in the paradigm of "economies of scale" through his mass production innovations. "You can have any color you want as long as it's black." Around this paradigm has developed most of our current sets of legal, financial and accounting standards, and much of our management culture. Those standards and that culture were appropriate at a time when product and process life cycles were measured in decades. However, mass markets now have fragmented and gone global. Also, life cycles now have collapsed often to a few years, and a capital-intensive dedicated facility can become quickly obsolescent (The "Asian Meltdown"). Just-in-time delivery of a continually changing mix of customized products has become a measure of survival, and the old methods and standards have become a problem.

- A dedicated plant, producing obsolescent products, often continues to build inventories which (in current accounting methodology) appear on the books as assets, when they now are a liability.
- Just-in-time delivery of a changing mix of products based on a "common platform," requires design of flexible systems at the earliest possible stage of

development. The total cost of development and the reduction in time to market can be enormous.

Such flexible computer-integrated systems also can provide continuing incremental improvements of existing products, and allow rapid prototyping of new products. Such facilities now are being programmed to make hundreds of variations, with turnaround times between variations of a few seconds, and with similar costs for one or one hundred of a kind. This revolution in manufacturing has been made possible by major advances in robotics, electronics, sensors, and software, ("running all night with the lights off").

- o A flexible facility can allow companies to share time for intermittant production requirements at much reduced cost, and with expert managment --- the management of continuous change.
- o Inventory costs can be much reduced by just-in-time production and delivery.
- o Production can be continually adjusted for changing needs with consistent quality control and reproducibility.
- o High entry costs for new product prototyping and ramp-up can be much reduced over a plant operating at partial capacity.
- o "Micro factories" at colleges and universities, can provide services to local companies while training the engineers and technicians who will operate them later.
- o Geographicaly dispersed facilities can be programmed by satellite to make identical products for local distribution as needed.

It is important for the manager-champion of the innovation process to pay special attention to the downstream production requirements and involve the appropriate design engineers at the earliest possible time.

Intellectual Property Management

The aggressive management of an intellectual property function will be increasingly important, as the need to sustain a competitive advantage becomes more and more dependent upon owndership of knowledge-intensive, high value-added proprietary operations. In developing an intellectual property portfolio, three levels of protection should be considered:

o The first and most important level includes disclosures that are sufficiently unique that they would be very difficult to invent-around (for example, new compositions of matter, or highly novel software). These should be filed broadly in most countries.
o The second level includes strong "support" disclosures that can increase the breadth and depth of the basic disclosures, creating a maze of overlapping claims that would be difficult for an ethical competitor to infringe. These should be filed more selectively in only the primary industrialized countries.
o The third level includes "picket disclosures," primarily intended to prevent competitors from blocking access to niche uses or applications, often designed to force cross-licensing. These should be filed in the U.S. only.

Some countries do not allow process patents, so their registration in the U.S. protects the U.S. market, but also teaches competitors the technology for use in other markets. Costs of patent filing and annual maintenance are high. Therefore, any unused patents and those near the end of their patent life should either be abandoned or licensed if possible to others.

A patent owner <u>can</u> refuse to license a patent. In addition, there are no legal restrictions on the amounts charged for royalties; and the constitution provides for a patent <u>monopoly</u> for the life of the patent.

However, loss of patent rights can occur through misuse. For example, it is illegal to tie the sale of a patented product to an unpatented product, process or service, and such misuse is penalized by loss of the intellectual property rights. Also, a patent owner cannot prevent a licensee from also making and selling competitive goods, or require a licenseee to license another patent as a condition of receiving the first license.

- o The Justice Department antitrust suit against Microsoft has been partially based on the alleged use of pressure to prevent competitors from competing in areas patent-controlled by Microsoft.

Finally, the patent owner cannot require payments beyond the expiration date of a patent, or require fixing of prices, or an unreasonable grant back of technology developed by the licensee.

Personnel Management, and Technology Audits

A primary responsibility of the Chief Technical Officer is to make periodic audits of all technical functions. These include the time-critical availability of equipment, facilities, skills and funding for programs that have met corporate guidelines. Figure 58 summarizes the data needed for such an audit. However, this does not mean that every profit center must be fully equipped with redundant equipment, facilities and sophisticated skills, that may only be needed intermittantly. Certain analytical, pilot plant, and interim production facilities must be shared (wherever located and owned) through a centrally administered function. This function must be carefully indoctrinated to see itself as a "service" function providing both very personalzied and timely responses to requests. Conflicts for use of facilities can arise, and should be impartially settled as quietly as possible by the CTO or his service function manager.

Technology Audit Data

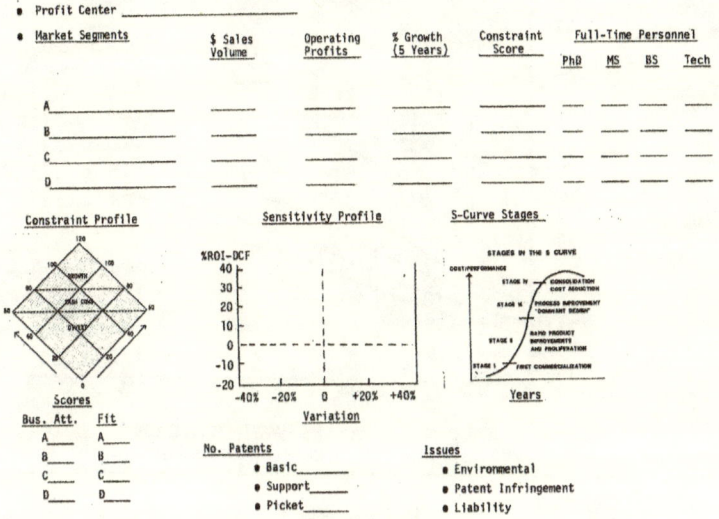

Figure 58

Of particular importance is the need for life-long continuous advanced skilling and reskilling of technical personnel. The salary maturity curves provide devastating evidence of industrial mismanagement in this area (Figure 59).

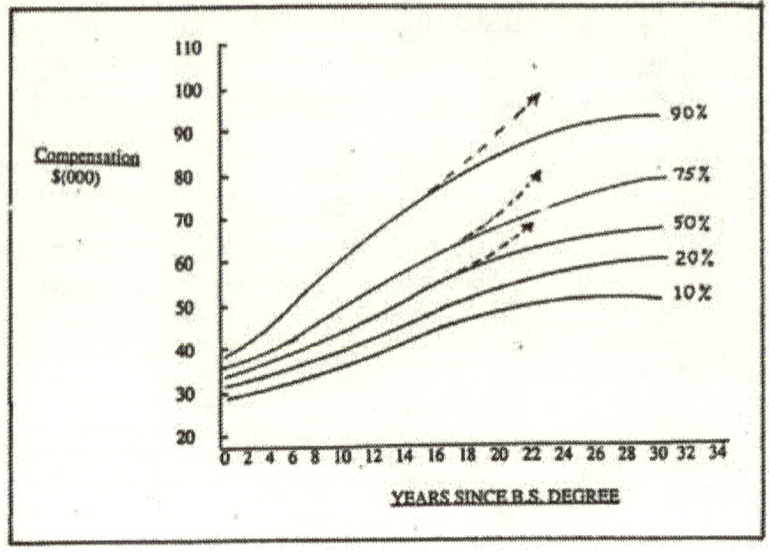

Figure 59

The American Chemical Society (ACS) and other professional organizations produce annual charts of the type shown in Figure 59. In the early years followiong a B.S. degree in engineering or science, salaries rise fairly steeply with experience, but then level off in the second decade and finally decline in the third decade, particularly in the 10% to 50% percentile groups. With good management, these curves should follow a course shown by the dotted line. In principle, no organization can afford many scientists or engineers who "choose to fall" below the 50% percentile. Good management in its own enlightened self-interest must make every effort to encourage all technical people (including technicians) to increase both their technical and business-related skills and knowledge, on an annual basis.

- o One company has put telecommunication dishes on the roofs of each of its 15 divisional laboratories and on the central research laboratory, connecting to local universities, for 8 hours a day reception.

Scientists and engineers enrolled in the classes being taught, can see and hear the professor who cannot see, but can ask and respond to questions to and from the students.
- The University of Phoenix and other universities now provide courses by satellite and over the internet for credit, or interest, including MBA and other management related studies.
- Many organizations also invite professors to provide in-house seminars on recent advances in areas of particular interest to the organization.

It is important to appreciate that technology now moves so fast that <u>any</u> set of skills now can become obsolescent within 5 to 10 years!

Environmental Audit

Equally important is a periodic environmental audit. An adversarial climate currently exists in the U.S. which seeks close supervision of almost all business activities, and the same concerns now are escalating in many other countries. In the U.S. since 1980 some 200,000 regulations have been prmulgated. Often these regulations carry severe penalties, and result in punitive class action suits as well.

Essentially "zero risk" now is the level of protection demanded by the neighbors of many business operations. Therefore any responsible management must carry out continual audits of all operations. Chemical, biochemical and materials-based industries have become particularly vulnerable, and waste control has become essential. The original "solution to pollution was dilution," or lagooning. This technique which runs diluted effluents into rivers, lakes and oceans is coming under increasing pressure. The Clean Water Act requires all bodies of water to be fishable and swimable. Industry compliance has been over 90%, but municipal compliance still is low.

Land fills have been the solution for solid waste, but these are progressively being exhausted or outlawed. As a result, incineration is increasingly used in the U.S., and is widely used in Europe. In Germany, waste is compacted and stored in exhausted coal mines. Bioremediation and total recycle methods have been piloted, and may eventually be mandated.

Hazardous waste currently is handled by deactivation and encapsulation methods where feasible. The eventual disposition of long-live radioactive nuclear wastes may find an acceptable long-term solution in encapsulation in a glass that is stable for 1000 years or more, and can be stored in deep salt mines with permanent monitoring. However, internal process improvements which result in higter yields of desired products and less by-product waste, can provide savings that pay for themselves many times over. These various options should be reconsidered on a regular basis, but the environmental audit requires a number of specific measures:

o A computerized data base is needed that provides detailed information about every by-product that must be disposed of.
o On-line automated analytical capabilities are needed to continuously monitor all process effluents for real-time deviations from acceptable limits.
o Incentives are needed for reduction of waste products. These incentives must be <u>immediately</u> awarded, be <u>tangible</u>, and be <u>measurable</u>.
o A vigorous public relations program also is required that involves community leaders, and the public. It should be designed to clearly articulate all the operating controls that have been put in place, the containment measures involved in case of an upset, and above all, the benefits that the business brings to the community (relative to possible risks).
o A detailed program should be put in place with time-based milestones to continually improve on each of these initiatives.

Summary

The effective management of innovation will be increasingly important to both corporate survival and to the entrepeneurial generation of new businesses. Unfortunately the disciplines needed are not generally taught in science, enginering, and MBA programs. This form of management now requires not only the traditional pursuit of incremental improvement in existing operations each year, but also requires equally vigorous pursuit of next-generation systems that can provide a sustainable competitive advantage.

However, the skills and resources needed to develop and commericalize next-generation systems frequently will not be present in one organization, and may be widely dispersed geographically. A critical path format will be required to integrate and coordinate this diversity of capabilities in real time, and the "manager-champion" must be competent both technically and as an administrator. Additional responsibilities involve a continual audit of the technical functions, the aggressive managment of intellectual property, and the life-long skilling and re-skilling of the personnel involved.

References

1. Francis Narin "The Increasing Linkage Between U.S. Technology and Public Science" Research Policy, Fall 1997: Chemical and Engineering News Sept. 1, 1997.

2. D.B. Merrifield "Strategies for Continuous Innovation" Research-Technology Management Jan. (1999).

3. D.B. Merrifield, William M. Evan, "The Department of Energy Superconductivity Initiative," Research-Technology Management, Nov.-Dec. (1998) pp 44-48.

4. D.B. Merrifield, "Corporate Renwal Through Cooperation and Critical Technologies" J. Resaerch-Technology Management July-August (1997) p 14-18.

5. D.B. Merrifield, "Industrial Survial via Management of Technology" J. Business Venturing, Vol. 3, No. 3, Summer (1988) pp 171.

6. Chemical & Engineering News July 27 (1998) pp 19-24.

KEY CONCEPTS TO REVIEW

1. In preparing a 5 to 10 year strategic plan in your company, you have been asked to identify possible next-generation systems that might meet projected growth and financial objectives, for a profit center with which you are familiar. Generate an audit of current capabilities, the limits for further improvement of the products involved, and the nature of breakthroughs that might be necessary to reach the objectives.
2. What is the status of the intellectual property invovled in this profit center? Should some of the disclosures be abandoned or licensed? What savings or profits would result?
3. For current R&D programs under development, have some elements in the critical path scheme progressed further than they should based on go/no-go milestones? What opportunities for strategic alliances exist that could potentiate the value of these programs?
4. What degree of top management support and direct involvement currently exists for these programs? What forms of communication might increase this support?

CHAPTER VII

LEGAL FORMS OF ORGANIZATION AND STRATEGIC ALLIANCE

Perspective

Form should follow function. But unfortunately in many organizations, the function needs to change, but internal bureaucracies both deny and resist the need, resulting in a primary cause of business failure. Belatedly, one strategy has been to downsize to the "core competency," but the core competency also may have become obsolescent, and adding more "bells and whistles" cannot salvage the past.

- o As low cost minimills stole about 40% of the steel business, the big steel companies belatedly adopted continuous casting and attempted to reduce costs.
- o Western Union was once the largest U.S. company, but it wouldn't believe that AT&T's phone system could replace telegrams.
- o A steam locomotive executive dismissed diesel-electric engines as no threat, just before diesels took the business.
- o And currently, distributed-power generation is steadily taking electric power business from the utilities --- and the Internet is displacing the media as a source of information...

Resistance to change in many large companies has been increased by the existence of largely independent divisions (fiefdoms) which jealously guard redundant and often under utilized capabilities.

Much more flexible forms of organization and management now are needed that can provide time-critical access to both those internal capabilities, as well as external resources when needed.

o   The overriding consideration is that a competitive advantage now will depend increasingly on the earliest possible market entry and a first-mover advantage.

Various forms of (global) strategic alliances often will be required, since few companies can hold captive all the skills, resources and contacts involved. Immediate access to needed capabilities, through collaboration, can be much more important than their ownership. However, historically there have been a number of barriers to collaboration.

For example, the fiercely independent U.S. culture often has seen collaboration "as some form of unnatural act" --- (in our company, we do everything ourselves!) Also, of course, collaboration requires specialized skills and management expertise to design, initiate, organize, and then operate different forms of alliance. This process, fortunately, is much better understood than widely taught or used. It involves well understood failure modes that can easily be avoided.

Another important barrier to collaboration has been the century old antitrust laws. Fortunately, this barrier finally was removed by the National Cooperative Research Act of 1984 (NCRA) --- landmark legislation which was unanimously passed by both the House and Senate. Since passage thousands of alliances have formed without a single legal challenge. This Act was further potentiated by the equally important Technology Transfer Acts of 1984, 1986 and 1989 --- and later further amended to include collaborative manufacturing. These Acts, for the first time, enabled industry to exclusively license and then develop and commercialize $billions of dollars of Federally-funded advanced technology. Previously, the populist concept was that any technology funded by tax dollars, belonged to all the people, and no one should own it. The result, of course, was that no company could justify significant investments in developing and commercializing a new discovery, and then have all its competitors follow in at a fraction of that investment. Consequently, only about 4% of 29,000 U.S. patents had ever been licensed on a non-exclusive basis.

These Acts, in combination with the 1981 Economic Recovery Tax Act (ERA), (which enabled private sector risk funding) marked a point of major discontinuity in the U.S. pace of innovation and in operational management. Hundreds of thousands of new businesses and millions of new jobs have been created in an historically unprecedented entrepreneurial revolution (the "American Miracle").

Alternative Forms of Organization

Historically, the most common form of organization has been a functional one (Figure 60)

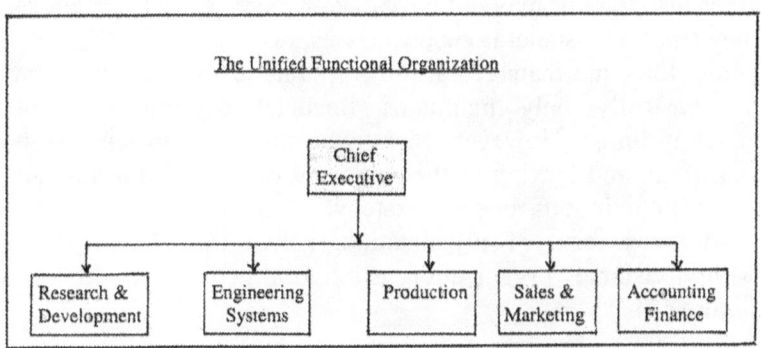

Figure 60

In this form of organization, none of the elements have bottom-line accountability as profit centers. Therefore, the corporate function must be highly centralized for command-control by the chief executive. Functional structures can work well for small businesses, but tend to be poor profit performers for larger companies.

A second form of organization is the holding company (Figure 61).

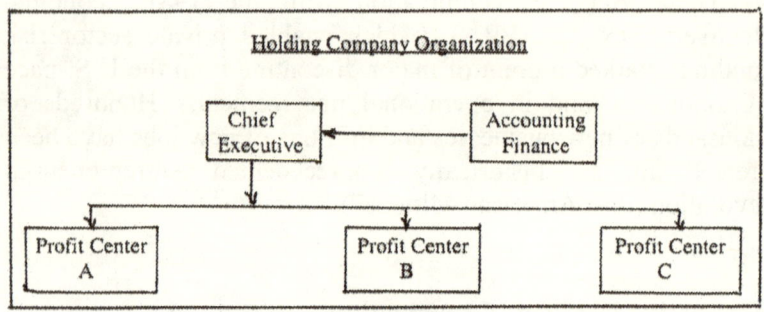

Figure 61

In this organization, the operating profit centers can be involved in either related or unrelated businesses (product lines), which also may or may not have one or more core competencies. They tend to be stand-alone businesses, responsible for their own bottom line, and managed at the corporate level by a small staff that basically only maintains financial controls over the operating units. However, operational management tends to be short-term, and lacking in the skills and resources to design and pursue a continuous renewal strategy.

A third form of organization, called the "M-form" for "Multidivisional" organization, is a hybrid between the first two (Figure 62).

MULTIDIVISIONAL ORGANIZATION
M-FORM

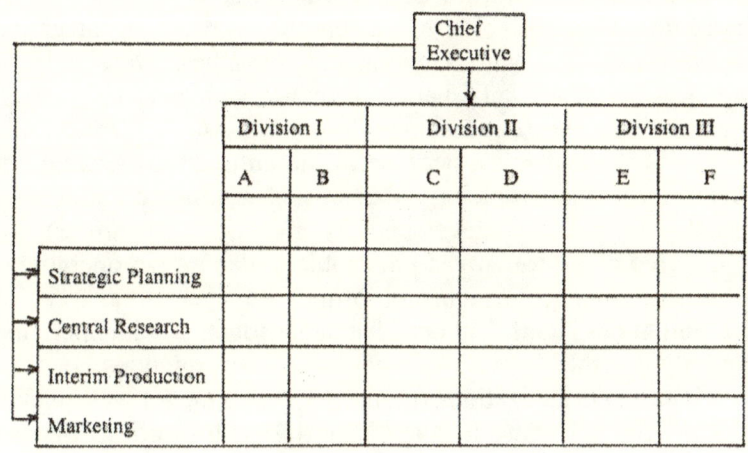

Figure 62

In this form of management, the operating units have accountability for their bottom line and are partially independent, in that each one makes a different set of products, or provides a service that is different from the others, but might share core competencies in marketing and manufacturing as well as technology. Corporate functions are charged with coordination of the cross-divisional needs involved. The strategic planning function is responsible for initiating an on-going process of growth and renewal. Frequently missing, is a sophisticated search-intelligence function operating on behalf of each profit center (A, B, C, D, and E). These three forms of organization tend to be internally focused and independent of outside complementary organizations. However, collaboration among complementary organizations, as opposed to mergers and acquisitions, increasingly will be a preferred form of management.

The Limited Liability Corporation

In the early 1980's, the Japanese Kieretsu consortial form of organization was able to assemble vertically integrated operations, which with Government subsidies, were able to capture major market shares in existing businesses, (steel, shipbuilding, textiles, machine tools, robots, semiconductors etc.). U.S. companies, because of the antitrust laws, were not able to form comparable organizations. The Limited Partnership model was initially developed by the U.S. Department of Commerce as a legal way to assemble collaborative operations. It has since emerged as a useful form of management as well. In addition, it has significant tax advantages together with operating flexibilities that preserve the basic sovereignties of the collaborating organizations (Figure 63). The model was quickly adopted by Genentech and later by many other biotech organizations, as both a method for raising risk funding, as well as accessing specialized skills and resources.

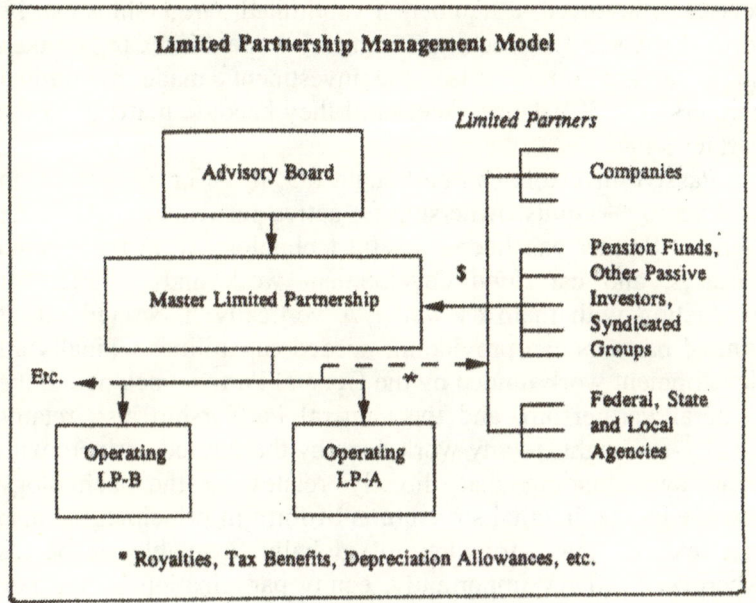

Figure 63

The General Partner (the Master Limited Partnership) runs the operation on behalf of any number of limited partners, who can own equity proportional to the value of their participation or investments. Because, by law, limited partners do not directly participate in day-to-day operations, they are insulated from both liability and antitrust considerations. However, as Advisory Board members they establish the mission and policy limits of the General Partner.

Limited partners can include companies with an active interest in the business, as well as passive investors, such as pension and venture capital funds, and Governmental agencies and laboratories. Once in operation the General Partnership becomes a conduit through which all depreciation allowances, tax benefits, and eventual profits flow back (without double taxation) to the limited partners. R&D investments made by the General Partner also are tax deductible by the limited partners against other passive income. If more than one product or service is involved, a number of sublimited partnerships can be formed. A sub-LP reaching commercial operation can be taken public at any time. Also, the investments made by limited partners are off balance sheet until they become material to the partner's P&L.

Passive investors can be bought out, by prior agreement, to capture 100% equity ownership for active participants. Also, the General Partner can license useful technology from the limited partners, and can fund development work and contract for production with them as well. A vertically integrated set of limited partners can provide all needed capabilities. Finally all development work funded by the General Partners belongs to the General Partnership, and the General Partnership also retains royalty-free rights to any work done by the limited partners with their own funding that directly relates to the technology involved. The internal structure is M-form in principle, but also can extend that structure to globally available resources wherever needed. Importantly, equity participation by the key active partners provides the most effective of all forms of incentive for success.

Failure Modes for Collaborative Efforts

To the degree that collaborations are perceived as "unnatural acts," even their initiation, can be a problem, let alone their organization and management. A number of important failure modes have been identified (Figure 64). In a vertically integrated organization, (inventors, component suppliers, an integrator and end users), the organization generating the innovation should be the initiator --- searching-out and enlisting the additional resources and funding needed. The managing director can be the innovator or the integrator with all active participants contributing skills and resources as agreed upon (in an S or C corporation or LLC organization) The "champion" is a very important person, who must be an excellent organizer-communicator, and have both technical and business competence. The job involves keeping all top managements involved and up to speed in terms of their timely allocation of resources agreed upon, and in terms of problems that arise. At least quarterly review sessions are required to check milestone progress, adjust time schedules, and rethink strategies if needed.

FAILURE MODES IN COLLABORATION

o   Lack of top management commitment and direct involvement.
o   Failure to structure the collaboration for maximum success incentives
o   Failure up-front to clearly define the specific contributions to be made by each participant, and when
o   Failure to find an exceptionally able coordinator-manager-champion

---

Figure 64

A Modern Marshall Plan for Developing Economies "INPACT" Organizations

Democracy cannot be sustained for long without first building a small business middle class that has a vital stake in both economic and political stability. Therefore, it is in the enlightened self interest of the already industrialized nations to facilitate the formation of new small businesses in the lesser developed countries (LDC's). Small businesses create most of the jobs. The United States, contrary to common perception, is primarily a nation of small businesses --- only 5% of the 18 million U.S. companies are publicly traded, and about 75% of the 80 million new jobs created between 1982 and 1999, have been formed by small businesses. These have been primarily responsible for the great strength and diversity of the U.S. economy.

A very successful model for achieving this objective was initiated by the U.S. Department of Commerce in the 1980's, called INPACT (International Partnership for the Commercialization of Technology). The objective was to form joint ventures between U.S. and LDC companies to jointly develop new innovative businesses. The pilot model was first organized with Israel, and was later "cloned" in India, Ireland, Chile and Finland. Most of the technology involved, surprisingly, was initiated by the LDC's, not by U.S. companies. However, the U.S. companies brought development expertise, management skills and access to the U.S. market, without which the projects would not have been successful. The Constraint Analysis has been used for initially screening these new opportunities.

The INPACT model (Figure 65) creates a small operations office in each LDC, whose first responsibility is to search out incipient new developments in that country, and then screen them for viability.

Promising innovations then are matched with a U.S. company through a counterpart U.S. organization, and joint ventures formed.

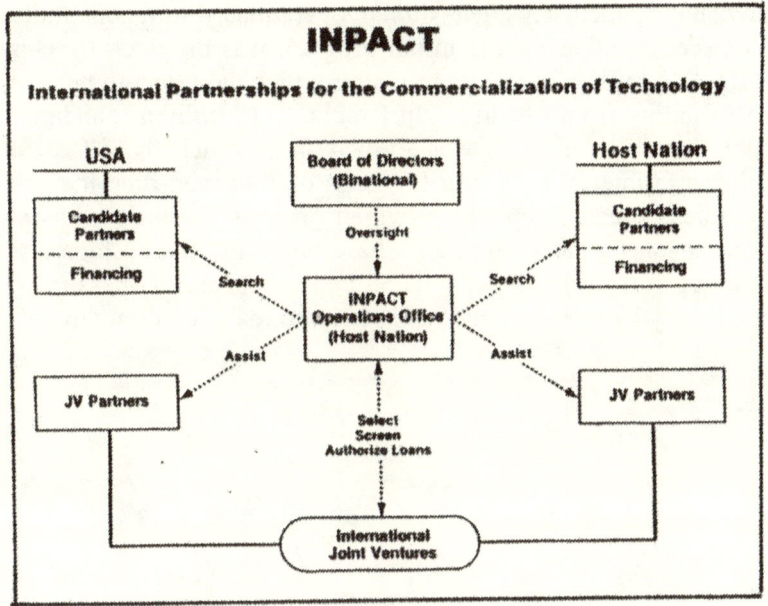

Figure 65

- In Israel, a small company had developed a drip irrigation system with plastic pipes, miniature motors, and water soluble fertilizers, but needed computer controlled operation. This was provided by a division of Motorola and the business now is a $500 million a year worldwide enterprise.
- In India, a small company had discovered a unique method for separating vegetable oils from high molecular-weight waxes in rice bran, a readily available raw material. India imports about a $billion dollars of vegetable oils for cooking, each year. A joint venture with Pennwalt provided the big centrifuges and the marketing-distribution capabilities needed, for this growing business.

Hundreds of similar examples have followed, and in India, the Industrial Credit and Investment Corporation of India (ICICI) now has funded ten other similar operations throughout India. The seed funding for the initial program was provided by U.S. AID ($20 million over 5 years), after which the program became self-funding from royalties. In Israel a $110 million foundation (half Israeli, half U.S.) was formed from which the $7 to $8 million in interest each year has been used to seed-fund the new ventures. Seed funds are provided on a 50/50 basis with the participants in each venture. These win-win relationships also open up foreign markets for U.S. companies, and by-pass many regulatory barriers --- nobody knows who really owns anything.

Summary

Older forms of management often have become incapable of the rapid change now required for survival. Also, periodic incremental improvements in existing operations no longer can assure a competitive advantage, and the radical advances now needed, cannot be managed by rigid organizations. In-house skills, facilities and resources now must be seen as "services," continually available on demand to an ever changing mix of task force managements, that in effect, contract for their use as needed. In-house ownership of all resources involved will become increasingly impractical, and therefore, collaborative forms of organization will be needed. Time to market and a first-mover advantage have become the dominant considerations. Off-balance sheet formation of limited partnerships have many tax advantages, as well as degrees of freedom, in accessing vertically-integrated capabilities on a global scale. The demise of both financial and economic sovereignty of the Nation State system will be one consequence of such cross-border alliances.

References

1. "The Innovator's Dilemma: When New Technologies Cause Great Firms to Fail," Harvard Business School Press (1998).

2. "The National Cooperative Research Act of 1984" (Public Law 98-467).

3. "The Federal Technology Transfer Act of 1986" (Public Law 99-502).

4. "The M-Form Society" William Ouchi, <u>Addison-Wesley Publishing Company</u> Reading, Mass. (1984).

5. D. Bruce Merrifield "A Modern Marshall Plan for Developing Economies" <u>J. Business Venturing</u> Vol 6, No. 4, July (1991).

IMPORTANT CONCEPTS TO REVIEW

1. Has form followed function in an organization with which you are familiar? If not, at what penalty in terms of decline or missed opportunities?

2. Where are the key barriers to change in that organization, and are there any "change agents" trying to make modifications? How are they treated?

3. How would you restructure the organization? What facts could you assemble to support your plan?

4. Is there at least one profit center that is amenable to change and restructure, as a model for others? As "the change agent" there how would you start? (Facts not opinions are necessary.)

5. Simulate an international model for one promising product line. What other organizations would you involve, and in what structure?

CHAPTER VIII

A GLOBAL VILLAGE IN THE THIRD MILLENNIUM

Perspective

In 1908, a Benedictine monk first published a study that describes a 500 year pattern in the rise and fall of civilizations. The last century in each of these "sesqui-millennial epochs" is always one of great turbulence, discontinuities and upheaval. But turbulence is the agent of change that causes the collapse of the existing obsolescent order, and then results in a tremendous rebirth or reawakening and the emergence of an incipient new order. The new order then dominates the succeeding 500 years (Figure 66). Since 1000 B.C., no new order has come into existence except around each 500 year node. The consequences for corporate management are understandably profound, but not necessarily clearly recognized.

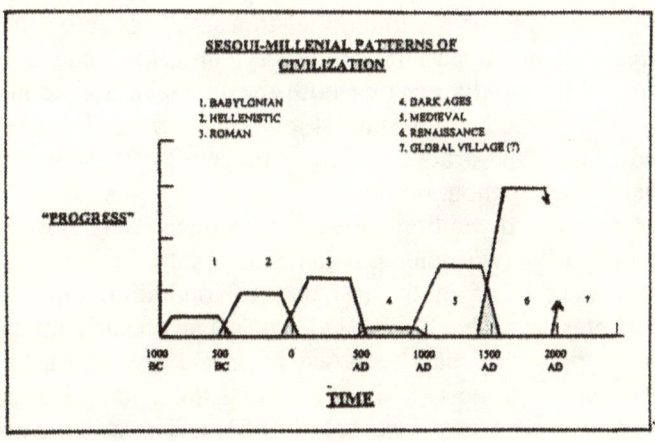

Figure 66

Historically, the new order that emerges in the first century of each new epoch, is followed by a period of chaotic growth in the second century, refinement and a flourishing in the third and fourth centuries. But then, bureaucratic rigidities repress needed changes, which lead to a new upheaval in the fifth century. The most recent 500 year epoch began with the Renaissance in 1500. It was triggered by Gutenberg's invention of the printing press in 1450. Within several decades, this invention had put some 10,000 monks out of business (copying books in Latin), and led to the collapse of the medieval order and church domination of society. In the Renaissance that followed, a Nation State system evolved, a great period of Reformation was begun by Luther, and the Industrial Revolution had its start, flourishing in the 18th and 19th centuries. But as the Benedictine treatise predicted, the 20th century has indeed been one of great turbulence. It has seen two World Wars, separated by the Great Depression, the collapse of colonial empires, the ethnic fragmentation of many countries, and the emergence of rogue states still involved in terrorism and the clandestine development of weapons of mass destruction --- hopelessly unproductive events. Moreover, just the last 30 years of this 500 year epoch, now have seen the astonishing creation of about 90% of all scientific knowledge. Advanced communications have tied the world together in real-time for the first time in history, stimulating thousands of cross-border alliances that are bypassing regulatory, language, and cultural barriers, while rapidly eroding both the financial and economic sovereignty of the Nation State system. This process is spelling the end of this "old order," and the emergence of a "new order," a global village without borders.

As if these disruptions were not enough, they have been compounded by two other phenomena. One of these involves the coincidental end of the last of the Kondratieff Longwaves (see Chapter I). The fourth and last stage of each longwave involves a period of massive downsizing and restructuring. This process started in the U.S. in the early 1980's, jump-started by the Economic Recovery Tax Act of 1981, and is well advanced. However, it has only recently begun in most of the rest of the world, causing major recessions outside the U.S. In addition, further compounding this difficult period for management, has been an incoherent set of U.S. fiscal, monetary and regulatory policies, which have generated a series of four year "boom and bust" economic cycles. Because of the size and great strength of the U.S. economy, these cycles affect all other countries as well, usually in amplified form. As a result, the process of management has been seriously complicated by this extraordinary confluence of (1) the end of a 500 year epoch, (2) the end of the last of the Kondratieff Longwaves, and (3) by incoherent U.S. economic policies. An acute awareness of these patterns is most importnat.

- o Organizations caught in the down drafts of a collapsing order, may not survive, but those that catch the rising tide of the new order can flourish.

Disruptive Monetary and Fiscal Policies

Monetary policy is administered by the Federal Reserve, an essentially autonomous agency that exercises its extraordinary powers, largely independent of either the Executive or Legislative branches of the Government. It is basically chartered to:

- o Ensure the integrity of the banking system
- o Protect the value of the dollar against inflation
- o Encourage economic prosperity

Because of its independent control over both the supply of money and principle interest rates, the Federal Reserve controls both the availability and the cost of capital, and therefore, in large degree, the rate and forms of investment allowed for U.S. businesses. No other agency has such invasive control over "industrial policy". This control, unfortunately, has led to a four year boom and bust cycle, that has been inimical to the global competitiveness of U.S. industry.

The Federal Reserve uses a combination of money supply and interest rates to control the rate of growth of the U.S. economy. Both are important. Therefore, a "monetary index" can be crated by using the ratio of M2 to the Federal Funds Rate (FFR). When this index (M2/FFR) rises, about a year later the GDP begins to rise, and traditionally, a year after that, inflation also rises. This cascade of events is illustrated in Figure 67, and the slanted lines illustrate the interdependence that results. Regression Analysis (Appendix II) shows a remarkable 99% correlation between Federal Reserve manipulation of the M2/FFR index, and the rise and fall of the GDP. The correlation with inflation is 95%. Curiously, the U.S. economy usually has peaked every four years, just at Presidential election times. A recession or serious downturn then follows about the time of the mid-term elections, when the Administration in office traditionally loses seats in Congress.

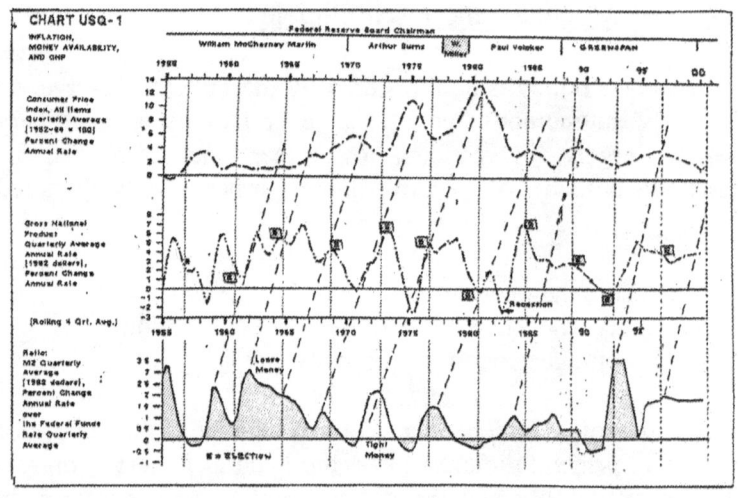

Figure 67

The Chairman of the Federal Reserve always is appointed in the third year of each 4 year Presidential term, which means that when the election switches parties, the new appointee overlaps three years into the next Administration.

President Carter failed to be reelected when a recession "coincided" with his election year instead of the usual mid-term period, and President Bush also was not reelected when the economy was only belatedly beginning to recover from the (unnecessary) 1990-1992 recession. Apart from the political consequences of manipulation, the economic uncertainty of a four year boom and bust cycle, is not at all conducive to sustained investments now needed for profitable growth in a hyper-competitive global marketplace.

Moreover, because of the enormous size of the U.S. economy, any downturn affects all other world economies, often in amplified form. Political instability and an increased environment for terrorism also can result. The pattern which follows each downturn, emphasizes the incoherent nature of the responses involved.

o As U.S. corporate sales and profits fall, unemployment also rises.
o Tax revenues then decline, but Government expenditures rise.
o Budget deficits balloon, and State and National debts increase.
o Taxes often then are increased to cover the shortfall in revenues, which further discourages investment and deepens the downturn.
o U.S. imports are reduced, causing downturns in other countries, which also then reduces U.S. exports to these declining economies.
o Protectionism raises trade barriers to discourage imports at "distressed prices" (called dumping).

At this point in each cycle, the Federal Reserve reduces interest rates and pumps up the money supply (by reducing the amount of reserves that banks must hold). This restimulates investments, and again --- with a year lag --- the economy begins to pick up. From a management point of view, an acute awareness of these Federal Reserve-initiated cycles has been very important.

Breaking the Cycle

The ability of the Federal Reserve to manipulate the U.S. (and world) economies has been diminished. About $1.5 trillion dollars are exchanged each day by world banks, and capital now flows with the speed of light wherever it is needed. Over $200 billion in foreign funds flow into the U.S. each year, making control of the money supply much more difficult. Also, the disinflationary effects of rapidly increasing productivity (Figure 68), combined with the enormous excess capacity worldwide in commodity businesses, has put a ceiling on inflation, and therefore on interest rates. Ironically, the 1990-92 recession set the stage for this new era. The recession was deeper and longer than usual, resulting in a longer than usual period of low interest rates.

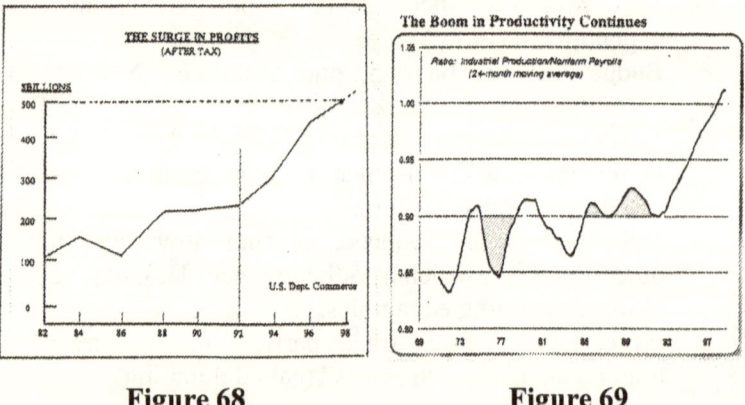

Figure 68 **Figure 69**

This allowed U.S. companies to make increased investments, resulting in much increased productivity and unprecedented profits (Figure 69) -- a virtuous cycle. Based on previous patterns, the 1993-94 surge in the GDP caused the Federal

Reserve to again decide to "cool" the economy in 1994-95, dropping the M2/FFR index to zero. In spite of this investments were largely sustained and have continued unabated. Because most of the new investments have been made in technology-intensive operations, the high-tech sector has boomed (Figure 70) relative to the total GDP. This sector will become more and more dominant, with or without the Federal Reserve, driven by advanced technology and rapidly vanishing borders in the emerging global village. These world markets, awash in liquidity, now primarily dictate both exchange rates and interest rates, as well as the availability of money. At the same time excess capacity in basic materials, capital goods, and other commodity businesses will require continued downsizing and rationalization in these areas --- the primary cause of the Asian meltdown and slow growth in Europe. In contrast, the market capitalization of technology-intensive operations, with proprietary character, have increased. (See also Figure 71.)

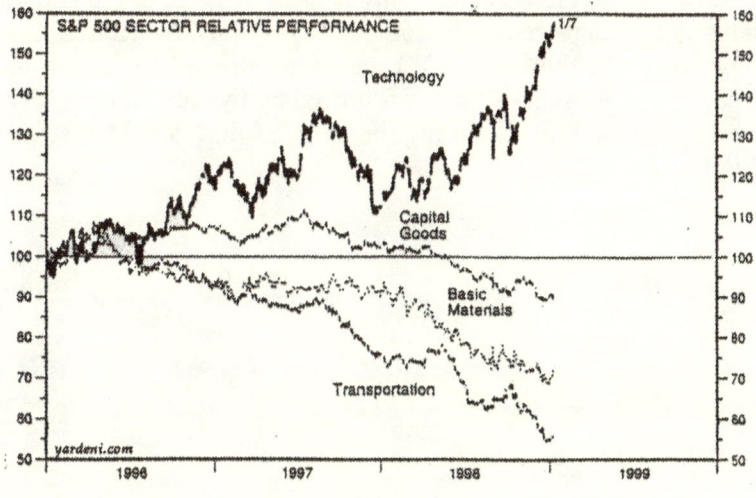

Figure 70

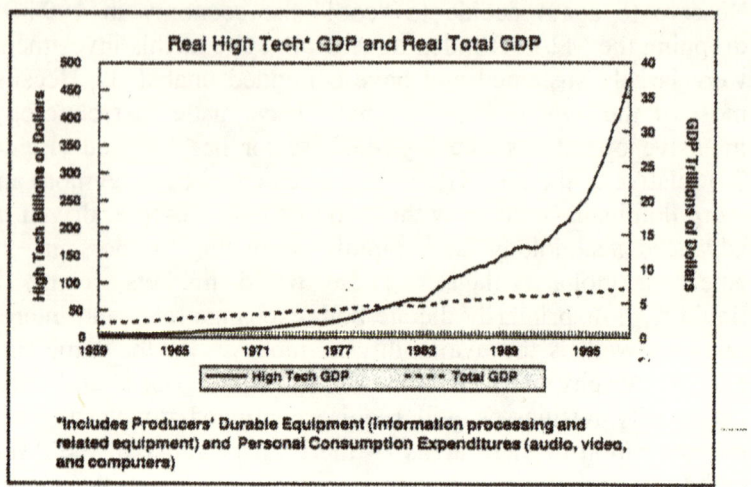

Figure 71

Previously, the U.S. Economy peaked in 1965, at the end of the second stage reinvestment period of the last Kondratieff longwave. The third (1965-75) stage typically resulted in excess capacity and erosion of profits followed by the need for massive downsizing and restructuring in the fourth (1975-90) stage, (Figure 72).

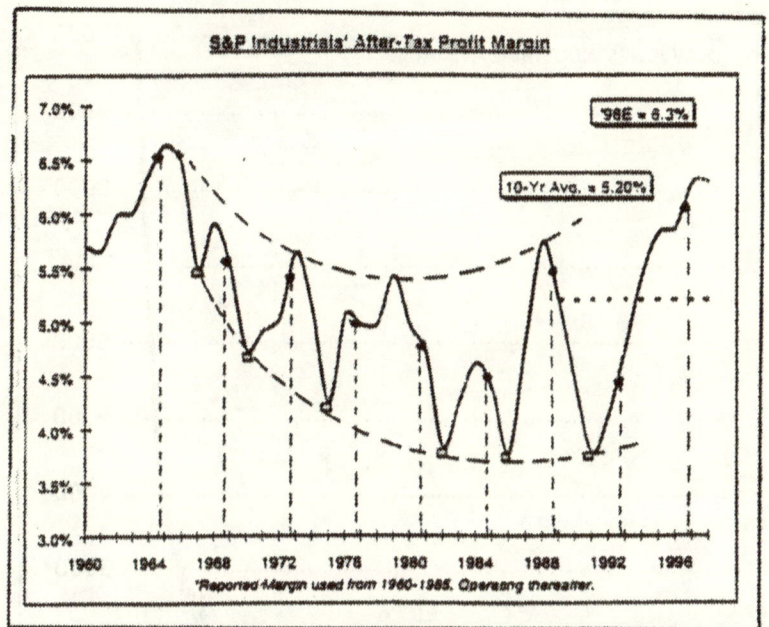

☐ Downturns and Recessions
• Presidential Elections

Figure 72

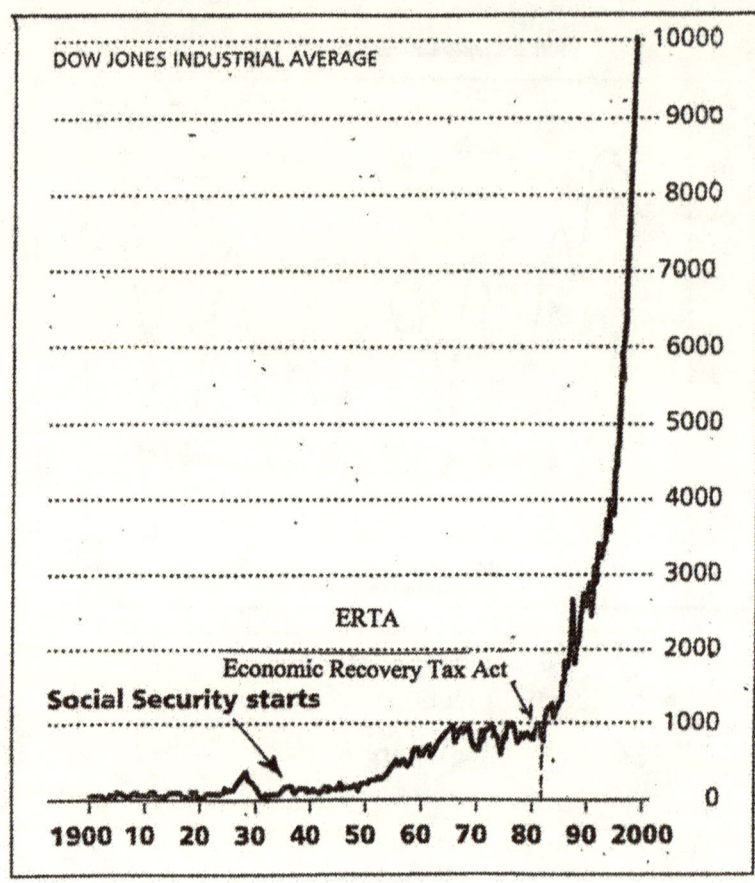

Figure 73

Fortunately, the Economic Recovery Tax Act of 1981 (ERTA), jump started the entrepreneurial revolution that has more than offset the downsizing process (Figure 73). Some 2 to 3 million new jobs have been created for 600,000 to 700,000 jobs lost each year. New business formations also have been sustained through the downturns, the source of over 70% of the new jobs. Fortunately, the strength of this self-regenerating process is so dis-inflationary that there never needs to be another induced recession. Moreover, budget surpluses can begin to eliminate the National debt and even better position the U.S. economy to expand worldwide. The primary role of management will be to continually develop new wealth.

The Emerging Global Village

The U.S. now spends over $35 billion each year for basic research, and over 6 times that amount for further development. This basic research investment is greater than all other nations spend combined and produces most of the seminal discoveries. This level of investment involves a unique technology-based infrastructure not currently matched (and probably unmatchable) by any other nation, in any reasonable time. Moreover, the consequences of these investments are exponential, because discoveries in different disciplines often interact in unexpected ways to produce surprise innovations, not at all anticipated in the original work. This phenomenon, is the primary driving force, ushering in the new "global era." Because it exists, and is primarily U.S. produced, the U.S. has unique responsibilities. The collapse of rogue states is preordained but may be violent. Moreover, the "changing of an order" never has been smooth and resistance to change is endemic. However, the forces of change are overwhelming in this epoch as they have been in previous epochs. For example:

- o The end of the "cold war" has released billions of people to compete, for the first time, in global markets, accelerating global competitiveness.
- o Instantaneous satellite communications have tied the world together in real time, and now will bring education, for the first time in history, to every corner of the earth, releasing latent genius wherever it may exist.
- o The "laptop" will soon be a high fidelity radio, TV, video-phone and workstation tied to no locality, and accessing almost any resource as needed.

- Biomedical advances will change the quality and length of life introducing ethical issues never before considered.

These and hundreds of other changes will proliferate. Moreover, because of its enormous size, strength, and advanced scientific capability, the U.S., of necessity, must be a primary "force for stability" --- catalyzing but not managing or even directing the global processes of collaboration which can bring progressive growth and increasing prosperity to many nations.

Summary

World civilizations now are at the end of a 500 year epoch which has been dominated by a social construction called the Nation State system, one which has been marked by incessant territorial, cultural and religious conflicts. Both the financial and economic sovereignty of this system now has been breached and likely will progressively dissolve into a borderless society. Rapidly advancing technology is the primary agent of change, tying the world together in real time and offering the promise of a vastly increased quality of life for its 7 billion inhabitants.

As a true global village begins to emerge, management will increasingly become the management of continuous change, alert both to the possibilities of Governmental interventions as well as to historically unprecedented opportunities for collaborative alliances on a global scale. Management structures must be highly flexible, and focused on continuous renewal through collaborative development of cutting-edge next-generation systems --- now uniquely possible.

References

1. Ralph Adams Cram, "The Great Thousand Years" <u>Univ. Press</u>, Cambridge (1918).

2. A Millman, "The Vandals Crown: How Rebel Currency Traders Overthrew the World's Central Banks" <u>The Free Press</u> (1995); Stephen Stamos Jr. Book Review <u>Money and Banking</u> Spring 1996.

3. Jay W. Forrester, Innovation and the Economic Longwave" <u>Management Review</u>, Vol 68, No. 6 pp 16-24, June (1979).

4. D. Bruce Merrifield, "Creative Destruction in the New Millenium" <u>J. Technology Management</u>, Vol 4, No. 1, pp 1-9 (1997).

5. National Science Foundation <u>Science Indicators</u> (1997)

KEY CONCEPTS TO REVIEW

1. Change is always resisted, sometimes bitterly. The first step is denial, the second, grudging acknowledgment and depression, before a positive pro-active response occurs. In an organization with which you are familiar, identify one or two areas of greatest weakness, and think through a strategy for accelerating the process of renewal from denial to positive action.
2. What emerging set of technologies is likely to force the decline of the above operation, and can you identify the source of the initiative?
3. Is a strategic alliance with the innovator of the new technology possible and at what penalty. Is this the least worst strategy?

APPENDIX I

A SUMMARY OF 500 YEAR EPOCHS

The world community now is at the end of the sixth great 500-year epoch, a pattern first described by a Benedictine Monk in 1908, and now going back 3000 years. In this remarkable sequence, no new order has ever come into existence except around each 500 year node. However, this may also be the last of these epochs, because technology-driven change now is too rapid and continuous to allow the previous types of bureaucratic and cultural rigidities to build to the point of violent upheaval. Nevertheless, from a management point of view, it can be helpful to understand these patterns, because the current incipient demise of both financial and economic sovereignty of the Nation State system, has precedents in other epochs.

The pattern from epoch to epoch is remarkably similar, and always ends in the fifth and last century with great turbulence and upheaval. The old order is destroyed, and a new order begins to emerge. The underlying driving force appears to involve the need for increased personal freedom, and for better access to perceived opportunities for both self-actualization and for increased quality of life.

Starting in 1000 B.C., the Babylonians conquered and dominated the Mediterranean shores for 500 years, until 500 B.C. But their control wavered and dissipated, when Philip of Macedonia (and the Greek phalanx), and then Alexander the Great began the aggressive rise of the Hellenistic culture. This remarkable period of civilization was centered in Athens and lasted almost to the beginning of the Christian era. Julius Caesar then conquered Egypt and Gaul, and later the Emperor Hadrian built his wall across northern England. The "Pax Romana" persisted until the Visigoths invaded Italy in 450 A.D. and corruption had weakened Rome. The great empire collapsed into oblivion as the Goths, the Vandals, the Huns, the Bergundians, and the Saxons from the north, overran Europe.

Civilization disappeared in blood and flame, ushering in a 500-1000 A.D. period, when Christianity was displaced by Muhammadanism. This period, called the Dark Ages, was chaotic and unruly. Momentarily, Charlemagne, under the banner of Christianity, pushed back the barbarians, only to be overwhelmed again by a new wave of Byzantine terror. However, Byzantium had already sowed the seeds of its own demise, and the Norsemen from Scandinavia, again under Christian banners, swept down to reconquer Europe and England (the battle of Hastings in 1066). Christian zealotry reached a peak during this 1000 to 1500 A.D. period, starting with the Crusades in the 1100's, and a 500 year era of feudalism arose. Fiefdoms provided both the economic and political structure for this (relatively) more stable period, in which Lords and their Knights controlled territories worked by serfs. The church was a dominant factor in this period, and the conservator of learning and culture.

However, in 1450 Gutenberg invented the printing press, putting some 10,000 monks out of the business of copying books in Latin. Also, gun powder mitigated the power of the sword, and the Feudal system collapsed. A great Renaissance of learning saw the formation of Nation States and much greater personal freedom enjoyed by a much broader spectrum of people in the artisans and guilds. The Roman church was challenged by Luther and Henry VIII split off the Anglican church in the great Reformation. Barriers to trade fell, making possible the onset of the Industrial Revolution in England, and a period of colonial exploitation. But again rigidities in political/economic structures, and growing awareness of inequalities of opportunity again have precipitated wars of conquest. The 1900's have seen, as predicted, growing turbulence and trauma, the collapse of colonial empires, the ethnic balkanization of many countries, two world wars, a 50 year cold war and a worldwide great economic depression.

Perhaps most remarkable of all, the last 30 years of the 20th century have seen the generation of about 90% of all known scientific knowledge. This phenomenon has for the first time in history tied the world together in real time, and precipitated a proliferation of cross-border alliances bypassing regulatory, language and cultural barriers. A global marketplace already has emerged with rapidly vanishing borders, spelling the incipient emergence of a new order, concomitant with the demise of both economic and financial sovereignty of the old order --- the Nation State system. Internet and satellite communications now can bring capital technology, and education (the schoolroom of one) to every corner of the earth. The ultimate effect will be orders of magnitude greater than Gutenberg's printing press, ushering in a unusual quality of life never before conceivable.

However, rapid change can be bitterly resisted inviting increased trauma, violence and terrorism. But the demise of rogue states is preordained, and weapons of mass destruction can be contained. Enlightened leadership is required, and this responsibility uniquely rests with the United States.

APPENDIX II

REGRESSION ANALYSIS DATA FOR MONETARY INTERVENTIONS

The data used to conduct the linear regression analysis on the effects of the monetary policy upon Gross National Product (GNP) and inflation were as follows:

<u>Monetary Index</u> The yearly percentage change in M2 (in 1982 dollars) to the Federal Funds Rate in October of the years 1954-1985.

<u>GNP</u> The GNP percentage change from previous year - fourth quarter 1955-1986.

<u>Inflation</u> The Consumer Price Index (CPI) averaged for the years 1956-1987 based upon the four reported quarterly statistics.

As stated in the body of this paper, the ratio of M2 to Federal Funds Rate is a monetary index reflecting the Federal Reserve's monetary policy. The purpose of this analysis is to show that changes in the index are indeed significant factors in the resultant changes observed in GNP and inflation one year and two years later respectively. For example, the 1954 monetary index changes affected the 1955 GNP figure and the 1956 inflation figure.

<u>Monetary Index vs. GNP</u>

Exhibit I is a plot of the thirty-two data points showing monetary index changes (1954- 1985) against changes in GNP (1955-1986).

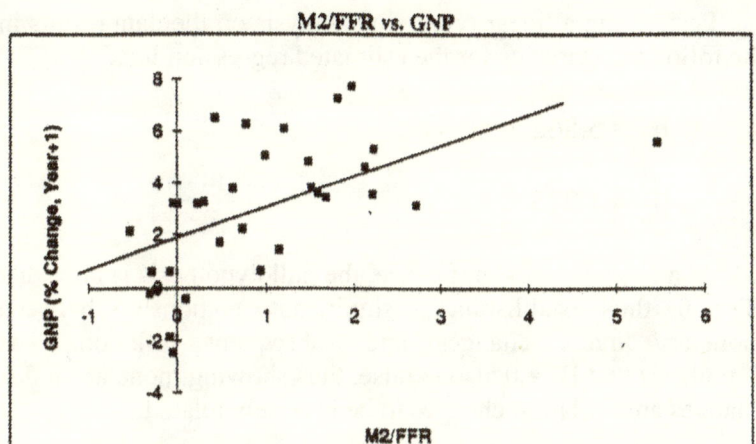

Performing a linear regression analysis on the data results in the following statistics:

b = 1.913   r = .212

b - 1.174   t = 3.652

Exhibit 1 shows the estimated regression line.

At a 1% level of significance, the null hypothesis is false that B = 0, thus establishing a significant relationship between monetary index changes and subsequent GNP changes. The hypothesis that B = 0 also is false, thus showing monetary index changes and GNP changes to be directly related.

Monetary Index vs. Inflation

Exhibit 2 is a plot of the thirty-two data points showing monetary index changes (1954-1985) against changes in inflation (1956-1987).

Performing a linear regression analysis on the data results in the following statistics for the estimated regression line:

b = 5.862

b = 1.275

At a 5% level of significance, the null hypothesis is false that B = 0, thus establishing a significant relationship between monetary index changes and subsequent inflation. The hypothesis that B = 0 also is false, thus showing monetary index changes and inflation changes to be inversely related.

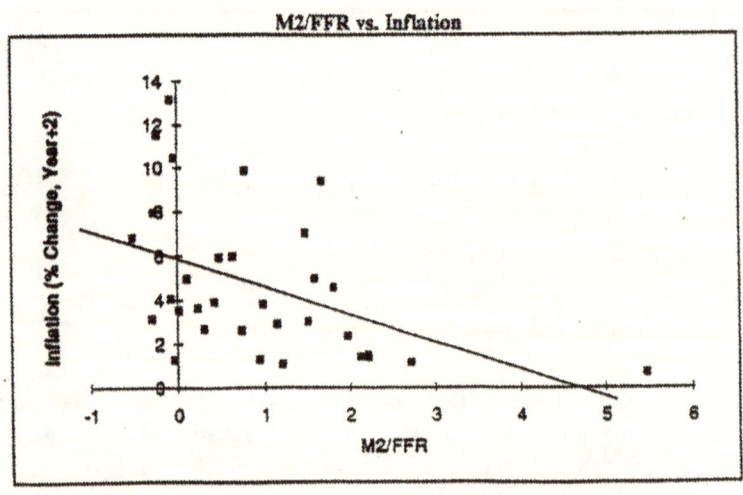

Conclusion

This simple linear regression analysis shows that the monetary model proposed does indeed have statistical significance. Changes in monetary policy over the past 30 years have significantly affected both GNP and inflation.

The coefficient of determination in these analyses (r) was .307 for GNP and .212 for inflation. For the period covered, this statistic reveals that, on average, monetary policy has explained almost one-third of the variance in a following year's GNP growth and over 20% of the variance in the inflation rate two years beyond. Given the hundreds of factors involved in GNP calculations and affecting inflation, the likelihood that any other factor could produce such an affect is vanishingly small.

APPENDIX III

BACKGROUND ON THE FEDERAL RESERVE

The Banking Act of 1935 restructured the Federal Reserve, removing the Secretary of the Treasury and the Comptroller of the Currency from the board, to "eliminate" political influence. However, this did not make the board independent. President Roosevelt appointed Marriner Eccles to the board Chairmanship, and Eccles was even more supportive of Roosevelt's economic policies than had been Henry Morganthau, his Secretary of the Treasury.

Later, during the Truman Administration the Korean War had ballooned inflation in 1951 to 8.0% and the Fed tightened credit, causing a downturn in the election year of 1952. A Republican, (Eisenhower) then was elected for the first time since 1932. Truman had tried to resist the Fed action, but the Congress supported the Fed against Truman's wishes, resulting in a "perception" of greater independence.

A mystique then began to grow that "the Fed performs arcane functions with total objectivity," and therefore, should not be "fooled around with by mere politicians or other mortals." Control then effectively passed to the Fed Chairman. Of course, in principle, the five district bank presidents, in alliance with two dissident members of the board, could override the Chairman and control policy. However a 1935 open market committee regulation was promulgated to the effect that no individual governor would represent his own district. This is still observed. Nevertheless, these "actors" help insulate the Chairman from criticism, since he can represent that decisions are not his alone.

Also, the Government always has perceived a need to have the confidence of the powerful financial community. One way to retain the desired confidence is to appoint a Chairman whom the financial community trusts to favor its interests. This tends to intimidate the Administration, since the "given word" is that any loss of approval by the financial community will result in a falling dollar and rising interest rates. The President and the Congress, therefore, have been limited in the choice of a Chairman. President Reagan's reappointment of Paul Volcker (a Democrat) as Chairman in 1983 was a direct consequence of such enormous pressure.

The Congress has both the right _and_ the responsibility to oversee Fed actions and policies. However, the secret way in which the Fed formulates policy, based on "passive data and weak theory," makes it difficult to do. As a result, the immunity of the Fed Chairman, allows monetary policy to be politically manipulated. The direction of manipulation depends upon the coincidence, or lack of it, of the political persuasions of the incumbent Chairman, and the Administration in office. Republican Chairmen were incumbent during the Nixon, Ford, and Carter Administrations, but a Democrat was the incumbent for the Reagan Administration. It was the national interest that suffered.

The national interest requires a stable and predictable monetary policy, which provides a climate for time-critical sustained investment. During the last two decades Fed policy has been highly unstable, unpredictable and inflationary on average. Moreover, tax and spend fiscal policies have been "out of sync" as well, partly because of overreaction to oscillating monetary policies. The U.S. has a unique responsibility to maintain monetary stability since the $7.5 trillion U.S economy tends to drive all economies in an interdependent global marketplace.

www.ingramcontent.com/pod-product-compliance
Lightning Source LLC
Chambersburg PA
CBHW031049180526
45163CB00002BA/748